SORROWS OF STEPHEN

SORROWS OF

STEPHEN by Peter Parnell

NELSON DOUBLEDAY, INC.
Garden City, New York

For my parents.

AUTHOR'S NOTE

The author wishes to thank Israel Horovitz
and the members of the New York Playwrights
Lab at the Actors Studio for their support
and encouragement through the early drafts
of *Sorrows of Stephen*.

Sorrows of Stephen opened on November 20, 1979, at the Theatre Caberet/The Public Theatre. It was presented by Joseph Papp and the New York Shakespeare Festival. Direction was by Sheldon Larry, setting by Stuart Wurtzel, costumes by John Helgerson, and lighting by Dennis Parichy, with the following cast:

STEPHEN HURT	*John Shea*
BUM	*John Del Regno*
LIZ	*Sherry Steiner*
TAXI DRIVER	*Kathy McKenna*
MAN AT THE OPERA	*William Duff-Griffin*
WOMAN AT THE OPERA	*Barbara Williams*
WILLIAM	*Richard Backus*
WAITRESS	*Anne DeSalvo*
CHRISTINE	*Pamela Reed*

It was previously presented in a workshop production, which opened on October 23, 1979, at the Other Stage/The Public Theatre, with the same cast, excepting:

WAITRESS	*Ellen Green*

SORROWS OF
STEPHEN

CHARACTERS

STEPHEN HURT

CHRISTINE

WILLIAM

LIZ

TAXI LADY (GINNY TREMAINE)

WAITRESS (SOPHIA PICKLE)

BUM (HOWARD FISHBEIN)

MAN AT THE OPERA

WOMAN AT THE OPERA

HOTEL DESK CLERK

The action takes place in STEPHEN HURT's apartment, and in various places in and around New York City.

THE SET

In the New York Shakespeare Festival production, a unit set looking not unlike a museum sculpture garden was employed. This unit was comprised of various modules that opened out effortlessly to reveal bed, bookcase, restaurant table, opera box, etc. as needed, thereby allowing for scene changes with a minimum of fuss. Something that keeps the action moving fairly swiftly is desired.

ACT ONE

SCENE ONE

(*City street. Stephen Hurt holding open umbrella in one hand. Reading* Sorrows of Young Werther *in the other. Carries box of chocolates and bouquet of flowers. Approach of car.*)

STEPHEN: (*Reads*)

"Why is it that whatever makes a man happy must later become the source of his misery? I often feel like tearing open my breast when I think of her. I have so much in me, and without her it all comes to nothing . . ."

(*Pause*)

Taxi! Hey taxi! I'm going to be late!

(*He goes back to reading.*)

(*Bum enters.*)

BUM: Hey, buddy, could you spare a dime?

STEPHEN: What? Yes, I think . . .

BUM: Say, don't I know you from someplace?

STEPHEN: I don't think . . .

BUM: Your face looks familiar.

STEPHEN: Does it?

BUM: Herman Melville High School, Class of '66?

STEPHEN: Yes.

BUM: Are you Stephen Hurt?

STEPHEN: Oh. Hi!

BUM: Hi.

STEPHEN: How are you?

BUM: Fine. You?

STEPHEN: Fine, fine. I'm just waiting for a taxi.

BUM: Really?

STEPHEN: Yes.

BUM: They're tough to get sometimes.

STEPHEN: *That's* true.

(*Pause*)

What's your name again?

BUM: Howard Fishbein.

STEPHEN: Howard Fishbein . . .

BUM: We were in Phys. Ed. together. I used to beat you up after class.

STEPHEN: Of course! Howard! It's you!

(*They embrace.*)

It's good to see you.

BUM: Same here.

STEPHEN: How are things?

BUM: Pretty good.

STEPHEN: That's good.

BUM: You remember those short stories I was writing?

STEPHEN: Yes.

BUM: Well, I sent a few in to some publishers and they expressed some interest. So I'm pleased.

STEPHEN: Good, good.

BUM: It's only a matter of time. How about you?

STEPHEN: Well, I'm working.

BUM: Uh-huh.

STEPHEN: I was in advertising for a while.

BUM: No kidding.

STEPHEN: Creative, you know.

BUM: Yeah.

STEPHEN: "It'll drive you crazy."

BUM: So I've heard.

STEPHEN: No, that was my ad campaign. For Datsun.

BUM: You're kidding. That was yours?

STEPHEN: Yes.

BUM: "It'll drive you crazy."

STEPHEN: It did. I'm in real estate now.

BUM: No kidding.

STEPHEN: Southern exposures my specialty.

BUM: How do you like that.

STEPHEN: It's okay, I guess. You've got to live in order to love, you know.

BUM: Was that one of yours, too?

(*Pause*)

STEPHEN: Care for a chocolate, Howard?

BUM: No, thanks.

STEPHEN: Not even a merron glacé?

BUM: I'm off sweets.

(*Pause*)

New girlfriend, huh?

STEPHEN: What makes you say that?

BUM: Or old one, I guess.

STEPHEN: We're very much in love.

BUM: Love is nice.

STEPHEN: Love is everything, Howard. We've been living together for six months.

BUM: How nice for you, Stephen.

STEPHEN: Yes. I think so, too.

(*Pause*)

Did you ever marry that girlfriend of yours? Marissa something?

BUM: Himmelstein.

STEPHEN: Himmelstein. Marissa.

BUM: She ruined me.

STEPHEN: That's a shame.

BUM: Why do you think I walk around with a gun in my pocket?

STEPHEN: A gun?

BUM (*Takes out gun*): One of these days I'm going to put it to my head.

STEPHEN: Howard, you wouldn't.

BUM: I might, Stephen. I might.

(*Pause*)

STEPHEN: Things are bad, huh?

BUM: The worst.

STEPHEN: Believe me, I understand.

BUM: Don't say that, Stephen.

STEPHEN: Why not?

BUM: Because I don't think you do.

STEPHEN: Well . . .

BUM: And don't be patronizing!

(*Pause*)

STEPHEN: I'm not.

(*Pause*)

Say, Howard, about that gun . . .

BUM: Oh, don't worry, Stephen. At the moment, it isn't even loaded.

STEPHEN: It isn't?

BUM: Here. See for yourself.

(*Hands Stephen gun*)

Yes, Himmelstein didn't make life easy for me. Upped and ran off with another man. Worked in the Dinosaur Room of the Museum of Natural History. Jurassic period. No, it wasn't easy to take.

STEPHEN: We are all victims of the heart, Howard.

BUM: You're telling me.

STEPHEN: Anyone else can know what we know, but our heart alone is our own.

BUM: That's very poetic, Stephen.

(*Stephen has put gun to forehead.*)

STEPHEN: It's Goethe, Howard. From "The Sorrows of Young Werther." Do you know Goethe?

BUM: Not personally, no.

(*Laughs*)

STEPHEN: I've just started reading it. And I think it's very important to remember, at times like this, what Werther said, if I can find it.

(*Reads*)

". . . We human beings often complain that there are so few good days and so many bad ones; but if our hearts were always open to enjoy the good, which God gives us every day, then we should also have enough strength to bear the evil, when it comes . . ."

BUM: That's very encouraging, Stephen.

STEPHEN: Is it? I hope it is.

BUM: Hey, aren't you waiting for a cabbie?

STEPHEN: Oh, yes.
(*calls*)
Hey, Taxi! Hey!
(*Screech of brakes*)
Well, I'll see you, Howard.
(*He shakes Bum's hand.*)

BUM: Be seeing you, Stephen.

STEPHEN: Here's a quarter.

BUM: Thanks, Stephen. You're a real prince.

STEPHEN: See you around!
(*Stephen exits. Pause. Stephen re-enters and hands Bum his umbrella.*)
Here. It's really coming down.

BUM: Thanks, Stephen. Thanks.

STEPHEN: See you!
(*Stephen exits.*)

BUM: Stephen Hurt.
(*Pause*)

The *Sorrows of Young* who?

(*Pause*)

Hey, my gun! Hey, mister! Hey, Stephen! He stole my gun!

(*Pause*)

How do you like that? . . .

(*Blackout*)

SCENE TWO

(*Stephen Hurt's apartment. Liz, packing. Stephen still wet. Chocolates, flowers*)

STEPHEN: I don't believe it.

LIZ: Believe it.

STEPHEN: Why are you doing this?

LIZ: Don't you know?
(*Pause*)

STEPHEN: I'm surprised.

LIZ: Yes.

STEPHEN: I thought things were, well, wonderful between us.

LIZ: That's because you always think that, Stephen.

STEPHEN: And it isn't true?

LIZ: No.

STEPHEN: Oh.

(*Pause*)

I brought you these.

LIZ: Thank you, Stephen.

STEPHEN: I hope you like them.

LIZ: They're lovely.

STEPHEN: They *are* lovely, aren't they?

LIZ: Could you put them with the others?

STEPHEN: Aren't you going to take them?

LIZ: There probably won't be enough room, Stephen.

STEPHEN: Oh. I guess not. No.

(*Pause*)

What will we do with the ficus?

LIZ: You can keep the ficus.

STEPHEN: But it's yours.

LIZ: Don't drown it.

STEPHEN: I won't.

LIZ: It needs watering once a week and plenty of sunlight.

STEPHEN: I'll just leave it for you, then.

LIZ: What?

STEPHEN: If you decide to come back.

LIZ (*Pause*): What time is it?

STEPHEN: Six o'clock.

LIZ: I'm late.

STEPHEN: Must you go right now?

LIZ: Yes.

STEPHEN: But we have tickets.

LIZ: Mmn.

STEPHEN: For the Met.

LIZ: Yes.

STEPHEN: With William and Christine.

LIZ: I know.

STEPHEN: Oh, good. So then you're coming then.

LIZ: Of course not.

STEPHEN: Oh. But. I thought.

LIZ: Stephen, I'm leaving you. Do you understand what that means?

STEPHEN: Yes, I know. I know.

(*Pause*)

Can you at least stay for dinner?

LIZ: I've called for a taxi.

STEPHEN: I'll invite him up.

LIZ: Ken will be waiting for me.

STEPHEN: Ken?

LIZ: From my office.

STEPHEN: You're moving in with Ken?

LIZ: He offered to help me.

STEPHEN: And so you're moving in with him?

LIZ: It's just temporary.

STEPHEN: Oh.

(*Pause*)

I thought Ken was gay.

LIZ: He is.

STEPHEN: Oh.

LIZ: At least, I think he is.

STEPHEN: Mmn.

LIZ: We'll find out soon enough, won't we?

(*Pause*)

STEPHEN: This is all happening a bit suddenly, isn't it.

LIZ: I suppose so.

(*Pause*)

STEPHEN: Oh, God.

LIZ: Look, it's not your fault, Stephen.

STEPHEN: Isn't it?

LIZ: No.

STEPHEN: You mean, you're not leaving me because of me?

LIZ: Of course I'm leaving you because of you.

STEPHEN: Well, then, it *is* my fault. You didn't even *look* at my flowers.

LIZ: I don't *have* to look at your flowers.

STEPHEN: Why not?

LIZ: Because you bring them every day.

STEPHEN: I thought you liked them.

LIZ: I love them. But when you bring them so often, they're no longer special.

STEPHEN: Why can't they *always* be special?

LIZ: Because then they'd be ordinary. They wouldn't be special.

STEPHEN: If you love something, it should always be special.

LIZ: That's been our problem all along, hasn't it?

STEPHEN: I don't think so. No.

(*Pause*)

I've never particularly liked the idea of living alone. It somehow doesn't suit me. But I always end up that way. I wonder why it is.

(*Pause*)

My last girlfriend did the same thing. Of course, we'd set ourselves up for it. We were reading Stendhal at the time, and I think she thought I was going to shoot her. Things got pretty dangerous toward the end of that novel.

LIZ: How did you finish it?

STEPHEN: I couldn't. Not after she left. I was too depressed.

LIZ: I meant the relationship. Not "The Red and the Black."

STEPHEN: Oh. I thought you meant . . .

LIZ: No.

(*Pause*)

STEPHEN: You need help with the books?

LIZ: I'm leaving the books.

STEPHEN: I'll help you.

LIZ: Forget them.

STEPHEN: Not even the Tolstoy?

LIZ: Especially not the Tolstoy.

STEPHEN: Don't you remember what we were doing when we first met?

LIZ: No.

STEPHEN: We had just started reading the Tolstoy. You were going with that physics professor. Your Alexi Karenin. And we wrote each other notes and met on subway cars. And I even challenged him to a duel.

LIZ: Which he refused.

STEPHEN: Too late. *You'd* already accepted.

LIZ: I remember that.

STEPHEN: Do you?

LIZ: Though I tried to forget it.

STEPHEN: Oh.

(*Pause*)

There is a wonderful moment toward the end, when Anna and Vronsky are in a carriage together on their way to St. Petersburg. They both know their great love affair is over, but they don't know what to say to each other. So they say nothing.

LIZ: They just sit together.

STEPHEN: Moving quietly through the ice and the snow.
(*Pause*)
I don't suppose you'd want to marry me.

LIZ: What?

STEPHEN: Since you're leaving.

LIZ: Are you joking?

STEPHEN: I was going to, Elizabeth.

LIZ: You're not serious.

STEPHEN: I bought the flowers and the chocolates.

LIZ: But you always buy the flowers.

STEPHEN: But I don't always buy the chocolates.

LIZ: Stephen, please!

STEPHEN: Would you, if I asked you?

LIZ: Don't ask me, Stephen. No.

STEPHEN: Oh, God . . .

LIZ: Do you want me to feel guilty?

STEPHEN: I want you to marry me!

LIZ: Why are you doing this?

STEPHEN: Because I don't want you to go!

(*Pause*)

Kiss me.

LIZ: Stephen.

STEPHEN: Please.

(*She kisses him.*)

Again.

(*She kisses him again.*)

My love.

(*Pause*)

LIZ: You like to kiss, don't you? Yes. You've been very good at kissing. You've been passionate, too. Yet shy. You've really been very shy. Maybe that's why I liked you. I've always liked shy men.

(*Pause*)

It's been nice, Stephen.

STEPHEN: Yes.

LIZ: It's been really very nice.

(*Car horn*)

There's my taxi.

(*Calls*)

I'll be right down!

STEPHEN: I'll call you.

LIZ: Let's wait a bit.

STEPHEN: Tomorrow.

LIZ: Whenever.

STEPHEN: Shall we have lunch?

LIZ: I'll be working.

STEPHEN: You'll take a break. I'll stop by.

LIZ: Enjoy your opera.

STEPHEN: Ken's number. Write it down.

(*She hesitates. Writes number.*)

I'll call you.

(*She exits.*)

I'll stop by.

(*Stephen alone. Looks about room. Goes to window. Watches taxi leave. Sees copy of "Anna Karenina." Opens it. Reads.*)

"Vronsky tried to remember her as she was when he saw her the first time—at the railway station—mysterious, charming, loving, seeking and giving joy, and not cruelly vindictive as he remembered her at the last. He tried to recall his best moments with her, but they were forever poisoned. He could think of her only as triumphant, having carried out the threat of inflicting upon him totally useless but irrevocable remorse . . ."

(*Pause. Throws down book. Looks at number on paper. Picks up telephone. Dials.*)

Hello? Is this Kenneth Holiday? This is Stephen Hurt. Elizabeth is on her way over to your apartment. But I want you to know, I love her. She's always welcome to move back in with me. And if she so chooses, I want you to set her free!

(*Pause*)

What? . . . Oh . . . Is this 538-0365? It is? . . . Doesn't Kenneth Holiday live there? . . . I see . . . Sorry. I'm sorry to disturb you . . . I must have copied the wrong . . . number . . .

(*Puts down receiver. Crumples paper. Sits depressed. Takes out gun from pocket. Puts it to his head. Smiles. Puts it away. Picks up* The Sorrows of Young Werther. *Reads.*)

(*Blackout*)

SCENE THREE

(*Sound of Randy Newman on taxi radio. Stephen in taxi. Young Taxi Lady at wheel.*)

STEPHEN: Could you change the station please?

TAXI LADY: What?

STEPHEN: The station. Could you change it. The curtain's already gone up, and they're broadcasting it. It's opening night.

TAXI LADY: Sure, okay.

STEPHEN: 98.6

TAXI LADY: Same as your body temperature?

STEPHEN: I'm running a little hotter right now.

TAXI LADY: Lucky for me.

STEPHEN: There's the overture. Could you turn it up?

TAXI LADY: What is it?

STEPHEN: Mozart. "Così fan tutte." Do you know the story, Miss (*Reads card.*)

Tremaine?

TAXI LADY: Call me Ginny.

STEPHEN: Miss Ginny Tremaine?

TAXI LADY: Can't say I do.

STEPHEN: Two young officers disguise themselves as Albanians and seduce each others' sweethearts.

TAXI LADY: Sounds racy.

STEPHEN: It is.

TAXI LADY: What happens?

STEPHEN: They get caught.

TAXI LADY: That's too bad.

STEPHEN: Yes.

TAXI LADY: I'd like to see it sometime

STEPHEN: You would?

TAXI LADY: Why not?
(*Car horn*)
Hey buddy, stay in your lane!
(*Honks her horn*)

STEPHEN: I've never been driven by a lady cabbie before.

TAXI LADY: You don't know what you've been missing.

STEPHEN: This town must be tough for lady cabbies.

TAXI LADY: Why do you say that?

STEPHEN: If you aren't careful.

TAXI LADY: Who isn't careful?

STEPHEN: Do men often come on to you?

TAXI LADY: Sometimes. But I've worked out a solution.

STEPHEN: What's that?

TAXI LADY: I only stop for those I like.

STEPHEN: That's good.

TAXI LADY: It's not too bad.

(*Pause*)

STEPHEN: Is that why you stopped for me?

TAXI LADY: You looked better than most.

(*Pause*)

I had one guy propose marriage to me right here. Between the zoo and a trip down to Port Authority. Actually proposed marriage.

STEPHEN: What did you tell him?

TAXI LADY: What do you think?

(*Car horn*)

Hey buddy, blow it out your ass!

STEPHEN: Those are the Albanians singing now. "La mia Dorabella capare non e . . ."

(*She blows her horn.*)

TAXI LADY: Oh yeah. Where the heck did you learn how to drive?!

(*Pause*)

Good thing I went through the Park.

STEPHEN: What?

TAXI LADY: That crosstown traffic is murder.

(*Screech of brakes*)

Well, enjoy your opera.

STEPHEN: I shall.

TAXI LADY: Or what's left of it.

STEPHEN: Listen, er, if you *are* interested, I happen to have . . .

TAXI LADY: You've got an extra for tonight.

(*Stephen nods.*)

Your girlfriend couldn't make it?

STEPHEN: Something like that.

TAXI LADY: I'd like to, Mr. . . .

STEPHEN: Hurt.

TAXI LADY: Hurt.

STEPHEN: Stephen.

TAXI LADY: Stephen. But I'm on till midnight. Another time, perhaps?

STEPHEN: *Sure thing*, Ginny. Maybe for "Pagliacci."

(*Hands her card*)

TAXI LADY: Realty agent, eh?

STEPHEN: If you ever need a place.

(*Hands her money. Pause. Taxi Lady suddenly leans forward and touches his cheek. Pause*)

If you pass by around ten, I'll stick out my arm.

TAXI LADY: If you stick out your arm, I just might pick you up.

(*Stephen gets out of cab.*)

STEPHEN: See you!

(*He exits.*)

TAXI LADY: Hey, don't forget your book!

(*He is gone. She picks up book. Opens to first page. Reads.*)

The Sorrows of Young Werther. ". . . And you, noble soul who feels the same longings that he felt, take comfort from his suffering, and let this little book be your friend when, because of destiny or some fault of your own, you cannot find a nearer and dearer one . . ."

(*Pause*)

Hm. Stephen Hurt. Realty agent.

(*Turns Music up. Car horn*)

Hey, buddy, blow it out your ass!

(*Blackout*)

Trio from *Così fan tutte,* by Mozart.

SCENE FOUR

(*Sound of Mozart. A box at the Opera. Stephen and William
seated behind a Man and Woman.*)

WILLIAM: Talk to her.

STEPHEN: What?

WILLIAM: *Talk* to her!

STEPHEN: In the middle of the last act?

WILLIAM: As soon as it's over.

(*Aria ends. Applause*)

MAN: Bravo! Bravissimo!

(*Stands*)

Bravo!

(*To Woman*)

He's wonderful, isn't he?

WOMAN: Yes.

MAN: Such incredible tone, such an emotional range! And the
depth of *feeling!* He's even better than he was a week ago . . .
He's the best I've ever seen him!

(*Pause*)

WOMAN: Which one is he?

MAN: Fabrizzi?

WOMAN: Yes.

MAN: The one who just walked off.

WOMAN: The one who took poison?

MAN (*Nods*): The one who took poison and just walked off.
(*Pause*)
He's coming back again.
(*Calls*)
Bravo! Bravissimo!

ALL BUT WOMAN: Bravo!

WOMAN: He's not bad looking.

MAN: No.

WOMAN: He's wearing a hairpiece.

MAN: He's supposed to be a romantic young hero. That's the part.

WOMAN: He reminds me of Manfred.

MAN: Who?

WOMAN: My friend. The young man who . . .

MAN: Oh. The unfortunate one.

WOMAN: Yes.

MAN: The one who tried to do away with himself.

WOMAN: The one who is dead.

(*Pause*)

He looks a little like him.

MAN: Where?

WOMAN: Around the eyes.

(*Applause*)

MAN: Bravo! Bravo!

STEPHEN: Bravo!

(*Woman turns and sees him. Their eyes meet. She turns back. Stephen sits.*)

She looked at me.

WILLIAM: When?

STEPHEN: Just now.

WILLIAM: Talk to her, then.

STEPHEN: I *can't.*

WILLIAM: Go up to her as soon as it's over.

(*Pause*)

STEPHEN: Do you have a piece of paper?

WILLIAM: No.

STEPHEN: How about a pen?

(*William hands Stephen a pen. Stephen writes on his program.*)
Does suffrit have two fs?

WILLIAM: Suffrit?

STEPHEN: Yes.

WILLIAM: Well, suffer has two fs. So I suppose suffrit . . .

STEPHEN: Has two fs, too.

WILLIAM: But fou has only one o.

(*Stephen makes corrections. Woman turns back to look at Stephen again. Their eyes meet. She looks away.*)

WOMAN: Let's go.

MAN: What?

WOMAN: I want to go.

MAN: But the last scene . . .

WOMAN: I want to leave now.

(*They start to depart.*)

STEPHEN: Excuse me, Madamoiselle?

WOMAN: Yes?

STEPHEN: You dropped this.

WOMAN: I did?

STEPHEN: Yes.

(*He hands her note.*)

WOMAN: Thank you.

STEPHEN: My pleasure.

(*She opens note. Reads it. Looks at him. Smiles.*)

WOMAN: Thank you.

(*She and Man exit. William smiles, pats Stephen on the back. Stephen sinks in his seat. Applause*)

WILLIAM (*Stands*): Bravo! Bravo!

(*Blackout*)

Finale from *Così fan tutte*, by Mozart.

SCENE FIVE

(*Restaurant. Stephen and William.*)

STEPHEN: Oh, God.

WILLIAM: What?

STEPHEN: I lost it.

WILLIAM: You did?

STEPHEN: Yes.

WILLIAM: Where?

STEPHEN: I don't know.

WILLIAM: At the Opera?

STEPHEN: I don't think . . .

WILLIAM: In the taxi on the way over?

STEPHEN: It must have been, yes.

WILLIAM: What's it called again?

STEPHEN: "The Sorrows of Young Werther." It's about a young nobleman who falls madly in love with his best friend's fiancée.

WILLIAM: Sounds wonderful.

STEPHEN: It is.

WILLIAM: What happens?

STEPHEN: I don't know. I haven't gotten to the end yet.
(*Pause*)
He shoots himself, I think.

WILLIAM: That's too bad.

STEPHEN: Yes.

WILLIAM: You'll have to pick up another one.

STEPHEN: It was Liz's copy.

WILLIAM: Try a different translation.

STEPHEN: Yes.
(*Pause*)

WILLIAM: Where is Liz, anyway?
(Waitress *enters*)

WAITRESS: Who had the salad nicoise?

WILLIAM: I did.

WAITRESS: You're the chocolate sundae?

STEPHEN: Mmn-hmn.
(*Waitress delivers food. Eyes Stephen. Exits.*)
Do you want the cherry?

WILLIAM: What?

STEPHEN: Do you want the cherry?

WILLIAM: No, thanks.

STEPHEN: Then I'll save it for Christine.
(*Pause*)
You did say she was meeting us, didn't you?

WILLIAM: Christine?

STEPHEN: Mmn.

WILLIAM: She's still editing Kornberg's boring new book.

STEPHEN: What's it called again?

WILLIAM: "Love Rites of the Yanomamo."

STEPHEN: It's wonderful about you two.

WILLIAM: Yes.

STEPHEN: Already engaged.

WILLIAM: Practically already.

STEPHEN: It's wonderful. How long have you known her?

WILLIAM: Almost six months.

STEPHEN: And you're already engaged.

WILLIAM: Practically already.

STEPHEN: It's wonderful!

WILLIAM: It happens.

STEPHEN: Yes.
(*Pause*)
I like Christine.

WILLIAM: She's great, isn't she?

STEPHEN: Yes.

WILLIAM: You don't really know her, do you?

STEPHEN: Well, no, but I know her well enough to like her.

WILLIAM: You do?

STEPHEN: Well, yes.

WILLIAM: Well, yes. I guess. You do.

STEPHEN: Of course, I've never really talked to her. We haven't ever really talked to each other. I mean, not *really*. If you know what I mean.

WILLIAM: Yes. I do.

(*Pause*)

She thinks of you as my romantic friend who falls in love with every woman he meets.

STEPHEN: She does?

WILLIAM: Yes.

STEPHEN: But that's not true.

WILLIAM: It is.

STEPHEN: It isn't.

WILLIAM: Well, *practically* every woman.

STEPHEN: You're the one who loves them and leaves them.

WILLIAM: Well . . .

STEPHEN: I just love them and they leave me.

WILLIAM: What do you mean?

STEPHEN: Too bad she had to work late.

WILLIAM: Who?

STEPHEN: Christine. She missed a great evening.

WILLIAM: Yes.

(*Pause*)

How are things with you and Liz?

STEPHEN: All right, I guess.

WILLIAM: Just all right?

STEPHEN (*Nods. Pause*): She's moved out.

WILLIAM: What?

STEPHEN: She's moved out.

WILLIAM: When?

STEPHEN: About three hours ago.

WILLIAM: Stephen.

STEPHEN: Yes.
(*Pause*)
I'm still in love with her.

WILLIAM: Of course.
(*Pause*)
Is she still in love with you?

STEPHEN: Mmn-hmn.

WILLIAM: Then why can't you two stay together?

STEPHEN: I wish I knew.
(*Pause*)
She told me she needed a change.

WILLIAM: Is that what she told you?

STEPHEN: Yes.

WILLIAM: And you believed her?

STEPHEN: Well, I didn't, no.

WILLIAM: You mean you disagreed?

STEPHEN: Not exactly. At least, I don't think I did. She was on her way out. I can't really remember.

(*Pause*)

I remember I felt like hitting her. I remember that.

WILLIAM: Did you?

STEPHEN: Of course not.

WILLIAM: You should've.

STEPHEN: She'd have had me arrested.

WILLIAM: She might have enjoyed it.

STEPHEN: Are you kidding?

WILLIAM: No. Some women . . .

STEPHEN: Not Liz.

WILLIAM: You'd be surprised.

(*Pause*)

I had a girlfriend once, it was all she talked about. How she wanted me to beat her. She went on for hours about it until I decided it was the most compassionate thing I could do. I brought her back to my place to put her out of her misery, but before I could lay a hand on her, she fainted. I felt a little disappointed, I remember.

STEPHEN: She's moved in with Ken.

WILLIAM: Who?

STEPHEN: Liz.

WILLIAM: Ken?

STEPHEN: From her office.

WILLIAM: Oh.
(*Pause*)
I thought Ken was gay.

STEPHEN: He is.

WILLIAM: Oh.

STEPHEN: At least, I think he is.

WILLIAM: Mmn. Well, she'll find out soon enough, won't she.
(*Pause*)
Talk about being masochistic.
(*Pause*)
Well, well. How do you like that.

STEPHEN: Yes.

WILLIAM: Are you all right?

STEPHEN: Mmn. How about you?

WILLIAM: Oh, I'm fine. Just fine. Christine—you know, she's like a goddess, really.

STEPHEN: Yes.

WILLIAM: She's impulsive, you know. Like you.

STEPHEN: Yes.

WILLIAM: I adore her. I idolize her, I suppose. And I've never particularly idolized women. Women are meant to be loved, not idolized.

STEPHEN: Do you think so?

WILLIAM: Don't you?

STEPHEN: Of course. Yes.
(*Pause*)

WILLIAM: She'd really like to get married.

STEPHEN: Who?

WILLIAM: Christine.

STEPHEN: Mmn.

WILLIAM: And God knows, I want to marry her, too. But it's a big step in a man's life.

STEPHEN: Yes.

WILLIAM: Not that I'm not up to it.

STEPHEN: Mmn.

WILLIAM: I just don't see any reason to rush into anything. I'm sure you can understand that, too.

(*Pause*)

That woman at the Opera tonight seemed pleased with your note.

STEPHEN: Mmn.

WILLIAM: Did you arrange to meet her?

STEPHEN: Tuesday at the Plaza.

WILLIAM: You think that's wise?

STEPHEN: Don't you?

WILLIAM: I mean, so soon after . . .

STEPHEN: Yes.

WILLIAM: You have to be careful not to jump into something just because you're feeling rejected.

STEPHEN: I know.

WILLIAM: You have to be careful when you get involved.

(*Waitress enters.*)

WAITRESS: Is everything all right over here?

WILLIAM: Excellent, yes.

STEPHEN: Thanks. Very fine.

(*Waitress eyes Stephen. Exits.*)

STEPHEN (*continued*): How are things at the station?

WILLIAM: All right. A man called up the other day and threatened to shoot himself over the air.

STEPHEN: Really?

WILLIAM: Yes. He wanted us to play "Fifty Ways to Leave Your Lover" and dedicate it to some girl named Marissa. He said he had a .45 in his mouth.

STEPHEN: Did he?

WILLIAM: I guess. I certainly couldn't understand what he was saying.

STEPHEN: What happened?

WILLIAM: We banned the song for a week. He's probably still waiting to hear it.

STEPHEN: He might have tried calling another station.

WILLIAM: He probably went out and bought the album.

STEPHEN: He could have just picked up the single.

WILLIAM: That's true. He wouldn't be needing the rest of the cuts, would he?

(*Pause*)

Stephen . . .

STEPHEN: It's all right. It's—I'm—all right.

(*Pause*)

Why don't you call and see what's keeping her?

WILLIAM: Yeah. That's a good idea.

(*He gets up as Waitress comes over to table.*)

Where are your telephones?

WAITRESS: Straight to the back.

WILLIAM: Thanks.

(*He exits.*)

WAITRESS: Are you finished with that?

STEPHEN: Oh, almost.

WAITRESS: I don't mean to rush you, but I'm going off-duty.

STEPHEN: Of course.

(*Pause*)

Where do you go?

WAITRESS: What?

STEPHEN: When you go off-duty.

WAITRESS: Home, usually.

(*Smiles*)

Unless something better comes up. Don't you want your cherry?

STEPHEN: No. You can have it.

WAITRESS: I'd love to. Maybe later.

(*Smiles at Stephen. Picks up William's plate, leaving Stephen's dessert. Exits. Stephen turns and looks in direction of Waitress. William returns.*)

WILLIAM: No answer. She must be on her way.

STEPHEN: That's too bad.

WILLIAM: Why?

STEPHEN: I've suddenly forgotten. I have an appointment.

WILLIAM: Now?

STEPHEN: Yes. I have to meet someone.
(*Gets up. Hands William bills.*)
I'll call you during the week.

WILLIAM: Right.
(*Stephen starts out.*)
Oh, Stephen—

STEPHEN: Yes?

WILLIAM: What's the name of that book again?

STEPHEN: Which book?

WILLIAM: The one you're reading. Maybe I'll pick up a copy for Christine. Sounds like something she might like.

(*Christine enters.*)

Christine! At last! We were just talking about you!

CHRISTINE: Hello, Stephen.

STEPHEN: Hello, Christine.

(*They kiss.*)

CHRISTINE: Were you just leaving?

STEPHEN: I'm afraid I have to, yes.

CHRISTINE: I'm sorry I'm late.

STEPHEN: Well, I'm off.

WILLIAM: Stephen.

STEPHEN: Yes?

WILLIAM: Are you sure you're all right?

STEPHEN: Mmn-hmn.

WILLIAM: Call me.

STEPHEN: I'll call you.

WILLIAM: Be careful.

STEPHEN: See you!

WILLIAM: Right.

(*Stephen exits. Christine smiles at William. Kisses him. William looks at Christine.*)

Well, don't just stand there, darling. Sit down and order something. It's about time.

(*Tries to get Waitress' attention, off*)

Miss! Oh, Miss!

(*Pause*)

Service is terrible these days.

(*Christine eats cherry.*)

(*Blackout*)

"Fifty Ways to Leave Your Lover" by Paul Simon.

SCENE SIX

(*Sound of alarm clock ringing. It is turned off. In the darkness:*)

STEPHEN: Calm! Calm! . . . Oh, du calme, Christine . . . We will find a way . . . Christine . . .

(*Lights up. Stephen asleep in bed. Waitress [Sophia Pickle] beside him*)

SOPHIA: It's Sophia, Stephen Hurt, Sophia Pickle. And I have to go now, too.

(*She gets up and starts to dress. Stephen rolls over and opens his eyes.*)

STEPHEN: What time is it?

SOPHIA: Eight o'clock.

STEPHEN: Where are you going?

SOPHIA: Home.

STEPHEN: It's early yet.

SOPHIA: My boyfriend is waiting for me.

STEPHEN: Your boyfriend! You didn't tell me . . .

SOPHIA: Would it have made a difference?

STEPHEN: Where does he think you've been all night?

SOPHIA: With you. Or someone like you.

STEPHEN: With me?

SOPHIA: Asleep with another man.
(*Pause*)
We have a very free relationship.

STEPHEN: That's nice.

SOPHIA: Yes.

STEPHEN: Why will he be waiting for you?

SOPHIA: He likes me to pour him his coffee.

STEPHEN: What are you, a waitress or something?
(*Pause*)
Don't answer that.
(*Pause*)
I'd like you to pour me my coffee.

SOPHIA: I can't. Find a waitress of your own.
(*Pause*)
What about your girlfriend?

STEPHEN: What about her?

SOPHIA: Didn't she pour you your coffee?

STEPHEN: I suppose, in a manner of speaking.

(*Pause*)

Actually, both of us drank tea.

(*Pause*)

SOPHIA: You didn't tell me you missed her.

STEPHEN: I don't.

SOPHIA: You do. You were saying her name in your sleep all night. "Be calm, Christine . . . it will be all right . . . We will find a way . . ."

STEPHEN: Did I call her Christine?

SOPHIA: Yes.

STEPHEN: Is that what I called her?

SOPHIA: You think about her a lot, don't you?

STEPHEN: I suppose.

(*Pause*)

SOPHIA: This is a very nice place you've got here.

STEPHEN: Thank you.

SOPHIA: You must do very well.

STEPHEN: What does your boyfriend do?

SOPHIA: He handles money.

STEPHEN: A financier?

SOPHIA: A teller.

STEPHEN: Oh.

SOPHIA: He works hard.

STEPHEN: Yes.

SOPHIA: Though maybe not as hard as you.
(*Pause*)

STEPHEN: Listen, I want to apologize . . .

SOPHIA: For what?

STEPHEN: For last night.

SOPHIA: What about it?

STEPHEN: The fact that I couldn't, well . . .

SOPHIA (*Shrugs*): It happens.

STEPHEN: Not to me.

SOPHIA: To everyone.

STEPHEN: Yes, but still . . .

SOPHIA: Was it the first time?

STEPHEN: That it happened?

SOPHIA: Yes.

STEPHEN: No.

SOPHIA: Oh.

STEPHEN: But I mean, it's not something I'm known for.

SOPHIA: Don't worry. I won't tell.
(*Pause*)

STEPHEN: I think it was my rushing into things that did it.

SOPHIA: Yes.

STEPHEN: The fact that I'd only just met you.

SOPHIA: Mmn.

STEPHEN: I mean, normally I'm used to rushing into things, but this . . . this was quite a rush!
(*Pause*)
I've had a lot on my mind lately.

SOPHIA: It's all right, you know. I understand.
(*Pause*)
A lot of men find me very attractive in the restaurant, and then, when they get me home . . . well . . .

STEPHEN: It's not that I didn't find you attractive, because I did, I do.

SOPHIA: This one man brought me up to his apartment and told me the only thing he really liked about me was my lips. He said a woman's lips were the most beautiful thing in the world. It was very nice for starters, but, well, nothing to make a night out of.

STEPHEN: I think your lips are very beautiful, too.

(*Pause*)

SOPHIA: You're feeling a little lonely, aren't you.

STEPHEN: A little, yes.

SOPHIA: Lost, almost.

(*Pause*)

Don't worry. Someone will find you.

STEPHEN: You think?

SOPHIA: You're too good not to be found.

STEPHEN: Good?

SOPHIA: Honest. Open. Innocent, almost. It's very unusual.

STEPHEN: Is it?

SOPHIA: Yes.

STEPHEN: Is it good?

SOPHIA: To be good?

STEPHEN: Mmn.

SOPHIA: Why not? I'd like to meet some more good men. The thing about good men is, often they're the most passionate.

STEPHEN: Are they?

SOPHIA: Mmn. When they're not acting good, that is.
(*Stephen looks bewildered. Sophia moves to bed. Kisses him.*)
Come on.

STEPHEN: What?

SOPHIA: Come here.

STEPHEN: But . . .

SOPHIA: We'll be all right this time.

STEPHEN: What about your boyfriend?

SOPHIA: There isn't one.

STEPHEN: There isn't?

SOPHIA: I made him up.

STEPHEN: Why?

SOPHIA: In case you didn't want to apologize.
(*Pause. She gets under the covers.*)
You're shaking.

STEPHEN: Yes.

SOPHIA: What's the matter?

STEPHEN: I'm afraid.

SOPHIA: Don't be.

STEPHEN: I am.

SOPHIA: Of what?

STEPHEN: I don't know.

SOPHIA: Being alone?

STEPHEN: Yes.

SOPHIA: But you aren't.

STEPHEN: No.

SOPHIA: You're with me.

STEPHEN: Yes.

(*Pause*)

But I know I will be.

SOPHIA: Alone?

STEPHEN: Yes.

SOPHIA: When?

STEPHEN: Soon.

SOPHIA: You mean later?

STEPHEN: Mmn.

SOPHIA: Later today?

(*Pause*)

STEPHEN: Yes.

(*Blackout*)

SCENE SEVEN

(*Lights up on lobby of Plaza Hotel. Stephen enters in rush. Looks around. No one waiting. Goes to Desk Clerk.*)

STEPHEN: Have any messages been left for me?

DESK CLERK: Who are you?

STEPHEN: Stephen Hurt.

DESK CLERK: Is that "hurt" as in wounded?

STEPHEN: I'm afraid so.
(*Desk Clerk checks.*)

DESK CLERK: No, sir. I'm sorry.

STEPHEN: That's all right.
(*He looks at watch. Shakes his head. Waits in lobby beside potted palm. Christine enters. Goes to Desk Clerk.*)

CHRISTINE: Have there been any messages for Christine Pane?

DESK CLERK: Is that "pain" as in hurt?

CHRISTINE: No. Pane as in window.

DESK CLERK: No; miss. I'm sorry.

(*Christine looks at watch. Shakes her head. Waits in lobby beside potted palm.*)

CHRISTINE: Stephen!

STEPHEN: Christine!

(*They kiss.*)

STEPHEN: What are you doing here?

CHRISTINE: Meeting William for lunch.

STEPHEN: At the Plaza?

CHRISTINE: He's been promising me.

STEPHEN: Really?

CHRISTINE: Yes. What are you doing here?

STEPHEN: Waiting for Miss X.

CHRISTINE: Really?

STEPHEN: Mmn.

CHRISTINE: Do I know her?

STEPHEN: I don't think so. William and I saw her at the Opera the other night.

CHRISTINE: Really?

STEPHEN: Yes.

CHRISTINE: Then I *don't* know her.

STEPHEN: No. Neither do I.

(*Pause*)

CHRISTINE: William's late.

STEPHEN: So's Miss X.

(*Pause*)

CHRISTINE: I rushed to get here.

STEPHEN: So did I.

CHRISTINE: The traffic was impossible. I kept telling the cabbie, go up Madison. Cut across 57th. Don't go near the Park. But you know cabbies, they never do listen. I don't think she knew where the Plaza really was.

STEPHEN: She? You had a lady cabbie?

CHRISTINE: My very first one.

(*Pause*)

She knew a lot about Mozart.

STEPHEN: Did she?

CHRISTINE: Yes.

STEPHEN: "Così fan tutte."

CHRISTINE: Pardon?

STEPHEN: "So do they all."

(*Pause*)

CHRISTINE: How about you?

STEPHEN: Yes?

CHRISTINE: Did you have trouble getting here?

STEPHEN: Oh. No. I walked.

CHRISTINE: You did?

STEPHEN: Yes. My office isn't far from here.

CHRISTINE: It isn't?

STEPHEN: 60th and Lex.

CHRISTINE: I thought you were over where William is.

STEPHEN: 56th and 6th?

CHRISTINE: Yes.

STEPHEN: No.

CHRISTINE: That's right.

STEPHEN: I used to be.

CHRISTINE: Before William was actually there.

STEPHEN: Yes.

CHRISTINE: *That's* right. So, in fact, you've never been very close to William.

STEPHEN: No. Not anywhere near at all.

(*Pause*)

CHRISTINE: Actually, you're probably closer to me.

(*Pause*)

I hate waiting for someone.

STEPHEN: So do I.

CHRISTINE: William is always late.

STEPHEN: Yes.

CHRISTINE: I think it's his subconscious desire to control our relationship, don't you?

STEPHEN: He probably just doesn't allow enough time.

CHRISTINE: When *I* was late to the restaurant the other night he gave me hell.

STEPHEN: Did he?

CHRISTINE: Yes.

STEPHEN: I was sorry I couldn't stay.

CHRISTINE: I was sorry I couldn't see you.

STEPHEN: I had this . . . date.

CHRISTINE: Of course. Things come up.

(*Pause*)

Do you think they'd mind if we went in and started without them?

STEPHEN: Who?

CHRISTINE: William and Ms. X.

STEPHEN: I don't think so.

CHRISTINE: I could write William a note.

STEPHEN: I could leave Miss X a message.

CHRISTINE: I don't think they'd mind, do you?

(*She goes over to desk. Stephen waits for moment, then follows. Christine writes. Stephen stands perplexed. Starts to write.*)

CHRISTINE (*continued*): Ready?

STEPHEN: In a minute.

CHRISTINE: I'll meet you inside.

(*She exits. Stephen writes note. Hands it to Desk Clerk.*)

DESK CLERK: Who is this addressed to?

STEPHEN: Better leave it in my name.

DESK CLERK: Pane?

STEPHEN: Hurt.

DESK CLERK: "Hurt" as in . . .

STEPHEN: Pain, yes.

DESK CLERK: Very good.

STEPHEN: No, wait. Never mind.

(*He takes back paper. Crumples it. Throws it in wastebasket. Exits in direction of Christine. Pause. Stephen re-enters, picks up crumpled paper from wastebasket. Puts it in his pocket. Exits.*)

(*Blackout*)

SCENE EIGHT

(*Christine and Stephen at end of lunch. Wine.*)

STEPHEN: Of course I feel bad. But what can I do?

CHRISTINE: It's not your fault.

STEPHEN: No.

CHRISTINE: Relationships are always tough.

STEPHEN: You're telling me.

CHRISTINE: I know, too.

STEPHEN: You've had many?

CHRISTINE: I've had my share.

STEPHEN: Then you know what I'm talking about.

CHRISTINE: I do.

STEPHEN: But yours didn't all end in disaster.

CHRISTINE: Most of them did.

STEPHEN: You mean you never went out with the men again?

CHRISTINE: Very few.

(*Pause*)

Of course, some of us wouldn't necessarily consider that a disaster.

STEPHEN: You wouldn't?

CHRISTINE: Knowing the men, I mean.

STEPHEN: You mean, knowing the kind of men you're talking about.

CHRISTINE: If you understand.

STEPHEN: I do.

(*Pause*)

CHRISTINE: I suppose that's one of the things that fascinates me about William.

STEPHEN: The fact that he isn't one of those kind of men?

CHRISTINE: The fact that he *could* be, if he wanted to. He's kind and considerate, but sometimes, he's just the slightest bit insincere.

(*Pause*)

It's not something I've ever told anyone else.

STEPHEN: Of course not.

CHRISTINE: It may be something I'm making up.

STEPHEN: No.

CHRISTINE: You mean you understand what I'm talking about.

STEPHEN: I do.
(*Pause*)

CHRISTINE: Do you know if he's ever hurt a woman?

STEPHEN: Physically, you mean?

CHRISTINE: Mmn.

STEPHEN: I think he has, yes.

CHRISTINE: Did you see it, or did he tell you?

STEPHEN: He told me.

CHRISTINE: Oh, then it probably wasn't true.
(*Pause*)

STEPHEN: Yes. He's been known to lie, too.
(*Pause*)

CHRISTINE: He's wonderful, William, isn't he?

STEPHEN: He's great. Yes.
(*Pause*)

CHRISTINE: I know he'd really like to get married.

STEPHEN: Mmn.

CHRISTINE: And Lord knows, I want to marry him, too. But it's a big step in a woman's life.

STEPHEN: Yes.

CHRISTINE: Not that I'm not up to it.

STEPHEN: Mmn.

CHRISTINE: I just don't see any reason to rush into anything.

STEPHEN: Yes.

(*Pause*)

CHRISTINE: Has he talked to you at all about me?

STEPHEN: What about you?

CHRISTINE: About him and me?

STEPHEN: Well, he likes you very much.

CHRISTINE: Yes.

STEPHEN: I mean, he loves you.

CHRISTINE: Mmn.

STEPHEN: He certainly intends to marry you at some point.

CHRISTINE: At what point?

STEPHEN: I . . . well, I don't really know.

CHRISTINE: But you think he's serious about it.

STEPHEN: Oh. Well, yes. I think so. Don't you?
(*Pause*)

CHRISTINE: I was really sorry to hear about you and Liz.

STEPHEN: Oh. Yes.

CHRISTINE: It's tough.

STEPHEN: It is.

CHRISTINE: I know.

STEPHEN: Yes.
(*Pause*)

CHRISTINE: It's important to try and live a little.

STEPHEN: Mmn.

CHRISTINE: You have to be independent, try to leave yourself open.

STEPHEN: I know.

CHRISTINE: Then something like this comes along and knocks you right down.

STEPHEN: It does.

CHRISTINE: But you can't tell yourself to stop feeling, can you?

STEPHEN: No.

CHRISTINE: You can't close yourself off to more love for less pain, can you?

STEPHEN: Mmn.

CHRISTINE: Well, I can't, at least.

STEPHEN: No. Neither can I.
(*Pause*)

CHRISTINE: It's important to let yourself be vulnerable. It lets you know you're alive.
(*Pause*)

STEPHEN: You know, I've always been attracted to a slight sense of danger.

CHRISTINE: Have you?

STEPHEN: Just a slight one. Haven't you?

CHRISTINE: I prefer mystery.

STEPHEN: I *adore* mystery.

CHRISTINE: Do you?

STEPHEN: Yes. Mystery is nice.

CHRISTINE: It seems safer somehow.

STEPHEN: It *is* safer, I suppose.

CHRISTINE: And I enjoy the excitement of it, too.

(*Pause*)

Have you been seeing a lot of women?

STEPHEN: A lot?

CHRISTINE: Yes.

STEPHEN: No. Not a lot. No. Since Liz left, I haven't felt much like going out.

CHRISTINE: You haven't?

STEPHEN: Not with a lot of other women. No.

CHRISTINE: What have you been doing?

STEPHEN: Reading, mostly.

CHRISTINE: That's nice.

STEPHEN: Yes. I just finished "The Sorrows of Young Werther."

CHRISTINE: You did?

STEPHEN: Mmn.

CHRISTINE: It's wonderful, isn't it?

STEPHEN: Yes.

(*Pause*)

I'm fascinated by it.

CHRISTINE: Are you?

STEPHEN: By its optimism.

CHRISTINE: Its optimism?

STEPHEN: Yes.

CHRISTINE: But it's supposed to be a tragedy.

STEPHEN: I know.

CHRISTINE: He kills himself in the end.

STEPHEN: But he does it because it's the only thing he can do! Not halfway through the story, Werther says, "I am amazed how I ran into this situation, with full awareness, step by step . . . How clearly I see it, and yet can't improve!" In other words, he hasn't deluded himself, because he knows he's deluded! So it's rather optimistic, really.

CHRISTINE: I've never looked at it that way before. It's exciting, isn't it.

STEPHEN: Very.

CHRISTINE: And dangerous.

(Pause)

I'd like to re-read it.

STEPHEN: You would?

CHRISTINE: Yes.

STEPHEN: Here. Take my copy.

CHRISTINE: I couldn't.

STEPHEN: Please.

(*He hands her copy of the book. Pause*)

CHRISTINE: Thank you.

(*Pause*)

Your Miss X didn't show up.

STEPHEN: No.

CHRISTINE: Maybe she didn't get your note.

STEPHEN: That could be.

(*Pause*)

It's been very nice talking with you like this, Christine.

CHRISTINE: For me, too.

STEPHEN: I mean, I've always liked you.

CHRISTINE: I've always liked you, too.

STEPHEN: But over the months, with Liz, and of course with . . .

BOTH: William . . .

STEPHEN: . . . the two of us never really had a chance to talk. I mean, not *really*. If you know what I mean.

CHRISTINE: Yes. Yes. I do.

(*Pause*)

STEPHEN: *My* problem is I assume the slightest show of affection in a woman to be the preamble to an act of love.

CHRISTINE: Really?

STEPHEN: Yes.

CHRISTINE: I don't think that's a problem.

STEPHEN: You don't?

CHRISTINE: Not at all. It sounds very endearing.

STEPHEN: Does it?

CHRISTINE: And rather dangerous, too.
(*Pause. William enters in rush.*)

WILLIAM: Christine . . .

CHRISTINE: William!

WILLIAM: I'm terribly sorry!

CHRISTINE: That's all right. We've just finished.

WILLIAM: Stephen!

STEPHEN: William.

WILLIAM: How did you two . . .

CHRISTINE: Look. Stephen just lent me his copy of "The Sorrows of Young Werther."

WILLIAM: I thought you told me you read it.

CHRISTINE: I have, but I'm going to read it again.

WILLIAM: Maybe I will, too.

CHRISTINE: Shall we run across the street?

STEPHEN: Would you like to?

CHRISTINE: Yes.

STEPHEN: So would I.

WILLIAM: Where are we going?

STEPHEN: To the park!

WILLIAM: But I haven't eaten yet!

CHRISTINE: Darling, there's a pretzelman on the corner.

(*They leave. Pause. Stephen returns. Puts tip on table. Sees Christine has left book. Picks it up. Christine re-enters.*)

Stephen!

STEPHEN: You left it.

CHRISTINE: That's why I came back.

(*He hands her book. She exits. Stephen follows.*)

(*Blackout*)

SCENE NINE

(In the Park. William and Christine strolling hand in hand.)

WILLIAM: You're not mad at me, are you?

CHRISTINE: Not really.

WILLIAM: Even just a little bit?

CHRISTINE: Maybe just a little.

WILLIAM: I told you I was sorry.

CHRISTINE: Yes.

WILLIAM: I called your office.

CHRISTINE: Mmn.

WILLIAM: You'd already left.

CHRISTINE: It's all right.

WILLIAM: I couldn't avoid it.

CHRISTINE: I understand. Really.

(*They stop. Sit on park bench*)

WILLIAM: Thank God you ran into Stephen.

CHRISTINE: Yes.

(*Pause*)

He's nice.

WILLIAM: Isn't he?

CHRISTINE: Very.

WILLIAM: I'm fond of him.

CHRISTINE: So am I.

WILLIAM: I thought you'd like him.

CHRISTINE: I do.

WILLIAM: You didn't know him very well, did you?

CHRISTINE: Just well enough to know I liked him.

WILLIAM: I guess.

CHRISTINE: But we never really had a chance to talk.

WILLIAM: I know what you mean.

CHRISTINE: Do you?

WILLIAM: Mmn. I think I do.

(*Pause*)

CHRISTINE: Where is he?

WILLIAM: Across the street.

CHRISTINE: Where?

WILLIAM: Talking to that lady jogger.

CHRISTINE: In front of the statue?

WILLIAM: Beside the statue.

CHRISTINE: To the woman in the green shorts?

WILLIAM: To the woman in the blue.

CHRISTINE: I see . . . oh, yes. I see him.

WILLIAM: Do you?

CHRISTINE: Yes. I do.
(*Pause*)
He seems very lonely, doesn't he?

WILLIAM: He is, I think. Yes.
(*Pause. William embraces Christine. They kiss.*)

CHRISTINE: Marry me.

WILLIAM: I will.

CHRISTINE: When?

WILLIAM: Soon.

CHRISTINE: I'd like that.

WILLIAM: So would I.

CHRISTINE: It'd keep me from feeling lonely.

WILLIAM: It'd keep me, too.
(*They embrace.*)

CHRISTINE: I see so much opening up for us.

WILLIAM: I want us both to be happy.

CHRISTINE: We know what we've got together. Why can't we get on with it?

WILLIAM: I want to.

CHRISTINE: So do I.

WILLIAM: Well then, we will.

CHRISTINE: When?

WILLIAM: Soon.
(*Pause*)

CHRISTINE: Sometimes I get scared.

WILLIAM: About what?

CHRISTINE: I don't know.
(*Pause*)
I'm afraid if we don't, something terrible might happen.

WILLIAM: Something terrible?

CHRISTINE: Something awkward.

WILLIAM: Like what?

CHRISTINE: I don't know.
(*Pause. Kiss. Stephen enters. Watches them*)
Stephen!

STEPHEN: Yes.
(*Pause. He exits.*)

CHRISTINE: Stephen, wait!

WILLIAM: What's the matter?

CHRISTINE: He looks upset.

WILLIAM: About what?

CHRISTINE: I don't know.

WILLIAM: He's probably thinking about Liz.

CHRISTINE: Yes.

WILLIAM: He's been depressed lately.

CHRISTINE: I know.
(*Pause*)

WILLIAM: Let's go.

CHRISTINE: Where?

WILLIAM: To see the monkeys.

CHRISTINE: Shouldn't we wait for Stephen?

WILLIAM: We'll run on ahead.

CHRISTINE (*Calls*): Stephen! We're going to the zoo!

(*They exit. Pause. Stephen enters. Sees book has been left on bench. Goes to it. Opens it. Leaves note inside.*)

CHRISTINE (*continued*):

(*Off*)

I forgot something. I'll be right back!

(*Stephen puts book down. Hides in bushes. Christine enters. Goes to book. Picks it up. Spots inscription. Reads.*)

"My dear Christine: See page 150, three lines from the top . . . Love, Stephen . . ."

(*She turns to page. Reads to herself. Pause. Holds book to herself. Smiles.*)

WILLIAM (*off*): Christine! Are you coming?

CHRISTINE: Yes! I'll be right there!

(*She exits. Stephen emerges from bushes. Alone. Pause. Smiles. Shoves hands in pockets. Exits after them.*)

(*Blackout*)

END OF ACT ONE

ACT TWO

SCENE ONE

(*Car horn. City street. William reading.*)

WILLIAM: "I can no longer help myself. I am in love with her. Sun, moon, and stars may continue on their course; for me there is neither day nor night, and the entire universe about me has ceased to exist . . ."

(*Calls*)

Taxi! Hey, taxi! I'm going to be late!

(*Pause*)

Christ. Where are they when you need 'em?

(*Approach of car*)

Hey, *taxi!* Stop for Chissakes!

(*William sighs. Checks watch. Shakes head. Bum enters.*)

BUM: Hey buddy, could you spare a dime?

WILLIAM: Not now. I'm in a hurry.

BUM (*Indicates gun in coat*): All right, hand me a few bills and we'll make it faster.

WILLIAM: Oh, Christ.
(*Hands over wallet*)

BUM: A coupla fives'll do me fine.

WILLIAM: You won't get away with this, you know.

BUM: Five.

WILLIAM: I never forget a face.

BUM: Five.

WILLIAM: There are ways, you know, of tracking you down.

BUM: Twenty.

WILLIAM: I'll need a little for cab fare.

BUM: Five.
(*Hands back wallet*)
Thanks.

WILLIAM: You took the twenty, too?

BUM: It's got four fives in it, hasn't it?

WILLIAM: Yes.

BUM (*Pause*): Say, don't I know you from someplace?

WILLIAM: No.

BUM: Are you sure?

WILLIAM: Yes.

BUM: Your face doesn't look familiar.

WILLIAM: No.

BUM: But your voice certainly does.

WILLIAM: Mmn.

BUM: Are you in radio?

WILLIAM: Yes.

BUM: You *are?*

WILLIAM: Mmn.

BUM: John Gambling?

WILLIAM: No.

BUM: Gene Klaven?

WILLIAM: I'm afraid not.

BUM: Don Imus?

WILLIAM: Sorry.

BUM: Dan Ingram?

WILLIAM: *Taxi!* Hey, *taxi!*

BUM: Joey Adams? Casper Citron? Barry Gray? Bob and Ray?

WILLIAM: Look, if you don't mind . . .

BUM: Bill Perky? Hey, are you William Perky?

WILLIAM: Very good.

BUM: William Perky! I'm Howard Fishbein!

WILLIAM: Nice to meet you.

BUM: Same here. You didn't play it.

WILLIAM: What?

BUM: You didn't play it.

WILLIAM: I didn't?

BUM: No.

WILLIAM: That's too bad.

BUM: Yes.

(*Pause*)

WILLIAM: I didn't play what?

BUM: The Paul Simon.

WILLIAM: The Paul Simon.

BUM: Yes.

(*Pause*)

I was the one who called.

WILLIAM: My God!

BUM: Yes.

WILLIAM: You're all right?

BUM: Mmn.

WILLIAM: We were worried about you.

BUM: I figured.

WILLIAM: We tried calling you back.

BUM: It was from a pay phone.

WILLIAM: Your girlfriend.

BUM: Marissa.

WILLIAM: She ran off with another man.

BUM: Dinosaur Room. Jurassic Period.

WILLIAM: That's too bad.

BUM: I'm getting sort of used to it by now.

WILLIAM: You are?

BUM: Yes. They're not worth dying over.

WILLIAM: No.

BUM: But they're certainly worth playing a song for.

WILLIAM: Yes.

(*Pause*)

BUM: Good book?

WILLIAM: Mmn.

BUM: "The Sorrows of Young Werther." You know, I heard something about that.

WILLIAM: Really?

BUM: I'd like to read it sometime.

WILLIAM: You would?

BUM: Yes.

WILLIAM: Be my guest.

BUM: Could I?

WILLIAM: Sure.

BUM: Thanks.

(*Pause*)

BUM (*Continued*): Say, you think I could borrow another quarter?

WILLIAM: Oh, sure, Howard, sure. Say, ah, about that gun . . .

BUM: This? Oh, this is just a pocket comb.

WILLIAM: It is?

BUM: Yes.

(*Shows him comb*)

I had a real gun, but some bum stole it. If I ever see that guy again . . .

(*Screech of brakes*)

Hey, here's your taxi.

WILLIAM: Oh, yeah, Howard, thanks!

BUM: I'll see you.

WILLIAM: You take care now.

BUM: I will.

WILLIAM: See you around!

(*William exits. Bum watches after him.*)

BUM: William Perky.

(*Pause*)

Hey, my comb! Hey, mister! Hey, thief! He stole my comb!

(*Pause*)

How do you like that . . .

(*Blackout*)

SCENE TWO

(*Christine in hotel suite, reading.*)

CHRISTINE: ". . . As you know me, you will understand only too clearly what attracts me to all romantic beings, and particularly to this one . . . This kind of love, this fidelity, this passion, is, as you see, no poetic invention. It is alive!"

(*Pause. Stephen enters.*)

STEPHEN: Ready?

CHRISTINE: Yes.

STEPHEN: Close your eyes.

CHRISTINE: Do I have to?

STEPHEN: Mmn-hmn.

(*Stephen kisses her. Produces toy.*)

CHRISTINE: Stephen!

STEPHEN: He's the one you liked, isn't he?

CHRISTINE: He's the one in the window!

STEPHEN: I begged.

CHRISTINE: They gave him to you?

STEPHEN: He was the last one left.

CHRISTINE: And look, he plays his drum.

STEPHEN: And look, he nods his head.

CHRISTINE: He's so soft and gentle! He's wonderful.

STEPHEN: Isn't he?

CHRISTINE: I love him.

STEPHEN: So do I.
(*He produces a cabbage.*)
Care for a cabbage, Mademoiselle?

CHRISTINE: Stephen!

STEPHEN: Yes!

CHRISTINE: Where did you . . .

STEPHEN: Shhh!

CHRISTINE: What?

STEPHEN: I stole it!

CHRISTINE: From where?

STEPHEN: The Oak Room downstairs!

CHRISTINE: Did anyone see you?

STEPHEN: That desk clerk.

CHRISTINE: Why did you . . .

STEPHEN: Don't you remember?

CHRISTINE: Did you give me a cabbage once before?

STEPHEN: No.

CHRISTINE: Did I tell you I liked cabbages once before?

STEPHEN: Of course not!

CHRISTINE: I give up.
(*Pause*)

STEPHEN: May I have this dance, Mademoiselle?

CHRISTINE: What?

STEPHEN: The first time that Werther dances with Lotte, he brings her a cabbage.

CHRISTINE: He does?

STEPHEN: Yes.

CHRISTINE: Oh.
(*Pause*)
No, he doesn't. He brings her an orange.

STEPHEN: He does?

CHRISTINE: Yes.

STEPHEN: You're right.

CHRISTINE: Yes.

STEPHEN: My God. He brings her an orange.

CHRISTINE: He doesn't bring her a cabbage.

STEPHEN: No.

CHRISTINE: Yes.

STEPHEN: Oh.
(*Pause*)
How could I make a mistake like that?
(*Pause*)
I'll have to re-read it.

CHRISTINE: Yes.
(*Pause*)

STEPHEN: Do you like it?

CHRISTINE: I *adore* it.

STEPHEN: It's wonderful, isn't it?

CHRISTINE: Yes. I don't want to finish.

STEPHEN: Maybe this time it will be different.

CHRISTINE: What do you mean?

STEPHEN: Maybe this time he won't shoot himself.

CHRISTINE: I doubt that.
(*Pause. They embrace.*)

STEPHEN: Clean again?

CHRISTINE: Mmn.

STEPHEN: You look clean.

CHRISTINE: I feel clean.

STEPHEN: You smell nice.

CHRISTINE: It's lemon.

STEPHEN: It's a clean smell.

CHRISTINE: Is it?

STEPHEN: Yes. It's nice.
(*Pause*)
My love.
(*Pause*)

CHRISTINE: To how many women have you said that?

STEPHEN: Not many.

CHRISTINE: A few?

STEPHEN: Very.

CHRISTINE: You mean it when you say something like that, don't you?

STEPHEN: Yes.

(*Pause*)

CHRISTINE: You're so different from William.

STEPHEN: Am I?

CHRISTINE: Mmn.

STEPHEN: How?

CHRISTINE: When William says something like "my love," it sounds like he's said it about a hundred times before. Not that he doesn't mean it. It just sounds like something he, well, thinks he's supposed to say.

STEPHEN: And when I say it?

CHRISTINE: It sounds like something you shouldn't have.

STEPHEN: Why?

CHRISTINE: Because. It sounds so . . . final.

STEPHEN: It *is* final. What's wrong with that?

(*Pause*)

My love, my love, my love, my love . . .

(*Christine laughs.*)

Better?

CHRISTINE: Thank you. Yes.

(*Pause*)

STEPHEN: My love.

(*Pause*)

CHRISTINE: This afternoon was wonderful.

STEPHEN: Did you like the movie?

CHRISTINE: I *adored* the movie.

STEPHEN: I love that movie. Catherine's such a wonderful creation, isn't she?

CHRISTINE: All three of them are.

STEPHEN: Wonderful, yes.

(*Pause*)

CHRISTINE: William wouldn't like that movie.

STEPHEN: He hates it.

CHRISTINE: He's seen it?

STEPHEN: With me. Twice.

CHRISTINE: He didn't like it?

STEPHEN: He hated it.

CHRISTINE: He probably thinks it's too frivolous.

STEPHEN: He thinks it's sentimental.

CHRISTINE: It's funny, isn't it?

STEPHEN: Yes.

(*Grabs cabbage*)

My love, your face is the face of a statue I saw once on an island in the Adriatic. It is like a force of nature. It is not just that you are beautiful, but that you are a woman. A woman whom all men desire. You are my queen, and I am your . . . cabbage.

(*They laugh.*)

Is it very different when you're with William?

CHRISTINE: Very.

STEPHEN: Nicer?

CHRISTINE: Different.

STEPHEN: But if you had to choose . . .

CHRISTINE: Stephen . . .

STEPHEN: I'm sorry.

CHRISTINE: We promised we wouldn't.

STEPHEN: Yes.

CHRISTINE: (*Pause*): It's very safe when I'm with William. I feel well taken care of. Not smothered, certainly, thank God. Just well looked after.

STEPHEN: And with me?

CHRISTINE: I feel stronger somehow.

STEPHEN: Because I seem weaker?

CHRISTINE: Because you are more gentle.

STEPHEN: And that makes you feel better?

CHRISTINE: Not better. Just different.

STEPHEN: Better than when you feel weaker?

CHRISTINE: Sometimes.

STEPHEN: Better than when you feel safe?

CHRISTINE: I don't believe that one can ever feel one thing ever totally.

STEPHEN: No?

CHRISTINE: Not for more than brief moments at a time.

STEPHEN: Then when you love someone . . .

CHRISTINE: It's "I love you *now*. I love you *now*. I love you *now*."

STEPHEN: And when you're engaged to someone . . .

CHRISTINE: It makes you feel safe.

(*Pause*)

STEPHEN: I love you now, Christine.

CHRISTINE: Yes.

STEPHEN: And now.

CHRISTINE: Yes.

STEPHEN: Now.

CHRISTINE: Yes.

STEPHEN: Now.

CHRISTINE: Yes.

(*Pause*)

STEPHEN: Now.

(*Pause*)

I'd like to make you feel safe.

(*Pause*)

In the past few weeks, I've felt more happiness than I'd ever dreamed was imaginable. I love you more than I've ever loved anybody!

CHRISTINE: Don't say that, Stephen.

STEPHEN: Why not?

CHRISTINE: Because nothing is ever that simple.

STEPHEN: Anyone else can know what we know, but our heart alone is our own! Do you know who said that?

CHRISTINE: Yes.

STEPHEN: And you believe it, don't you?

CHRISTINE: I'd like to, but . . .

STEPHEN: You do!

(*Pause*)

Are you afraid?

CHRISTINE: A little.

STEPHEN: Don't be.

CHRISTINE: I am. I don't want anyone to get hurt.

STEPHEN: Who'll get hurt?

CHRISTINE: I don't know.

STEPHEN: Then don't worry about it.

CHRISTINE: But somebody might.

STEPHEN: Don't worry about William. He'll survive it. I've known him longer than you have.

CHRISTINE: Yes.

STEPHEN: I've known him for a very long time.

(*Pause*)

It will be all right, Christine. Everything will be all right. We will love each other. And I shall take care of you. And we shall both, my love, be very, very . . . happy.

(*Pause*)

CHRISTINE: Oh, why do I find you so terribly attractive?

STEPHEN: I don't know.

CHRISTINE: It's your diffidence, I think.

STEPHEN: My diffidence?

CHRISTINE: Your romantic conviction is shot through with it.

STEPHEN: With a diffidence, you mean?

CHRISTINE: Yes. Or maybe it's simply your great capacity for love.

STEPHEN: That sounds nice.

CHRISTINE: It *is* nice.

STEPHEN: It *sounds* nice, anyway.

CHRISTINE: Yes.
(*Pause. They embrace.*)
It's time for me to go.

STEPHEN: Why.

CHRISTINE: I'm due back at work.

STEPHEN: Call in sick.

CHRISTINE: I can't.

STEPHEN: Take the afternoon off.

CHRISTINE: No.

STEPHEN: Run away with me.

CHRISTINE: I just did.

STEPHEN: Then get lost on the way back.
(*Pause*)
You haven't told him *anything* yet, have you?

CHRISTINE: No.

STEPHEN: Soon, I suppose.

CHRISTINE: Yes.

STEPHEN: Maybe I should . . .

CHRISTINE: No. I will.

STEPHEN: He's my friend.

CHRISTINE: He's my fiancé.

STEPHEN: Sooner or later, both of us . . .

CHRISTINE: We'll talk about it?

STEPHEN: Yes.
(*Pause*)
You mustn't feel badly, Christine.

CHRISTINE: No.

STEPHEN: It was something that had to happen.

CHRISTINE: I guess.

STEPHEN: It was fated. Beyond our control.

CHRISTINE: Mmn.

STEPHEN: We're talking about love, after all. Aren't we?
(*Pause*)

CHRISTINE: Yes.
(*Pause. Christine looks out window.*)
Oh, my God.

STEPHEN: What?

CHRISTINE: It's William.

STEPHEN: Where?

CHRISTINE: Outside, hailing a taxi.

STEPHEN: Really?

CHRISTINE: Yes.

STEPHEN: Are you sure?

CHRISTINE: He's talking to a bum.

STEPHEN: Can he see you?

CHRISTINE: If he looks up.

STEPHEN: Are you sure?

CHRISTINE: Yes.

(*Pause*)

What did he wear to work this morning?

(*Pause*)

Yes. It's him. Yes.

(*Pause*)

It's all right. They're saying good-bye now.

STEPHEN: He's got a taxi?

CHRISTINE: Yes. He's getting in.

(*Pause*)

STEPHEN: Come away from there, Christine.

(*Pause*)

Please. Come away.

(*Pause*)

Kiss me.

(*She kisses him.*)

Again.

(*She kisses him again.*)

Feel better?

CHRISTINE: No.

STEPHEN: Still frightened?

CHRISTINE: A little.

STEPHEN: Don't be.

CHRISTINE: I am.

STEPHEN: You're with me now.

CHRISTINE: Yes.

STEPHEN: Let me embrace you.
(*They embrace.*)
Let me make you feel safe.

(*Blackout*)

SCENE THREE

(*Stephen and William at the restaurant.*)

WILLIAM: I think she's been having an affair.

STEPHEN: Are you sure?

WILLIAM: No.

STEPHEN: *That's* good.

WILLIAM: But I think so.

STEPHEN: But you're not sure.

WILLIAM: But I *think* so.

STEPHEN: That's good.

WILLIAM: Why?

STEPHEN: Because. Maybe she's not.
(*Sophia Pickle enters.*)

SOPHIA: You boys know what you want?

STEPHEN: I'll have the chef salad.

WILLIAM: I'm not very hungry.

STEPHEN: Eat up.

WILLIAM: No. I'll nibble on some of yours.
(*Sophia smiles at Stephen. Exits*)
She's been meeting someone in the afternoons.

STEPHEN: How do you know?

WILLIAM: She keeps telling me she's been to the Museum of Modern Art.

STEPHEN: That's perfectly possible.

WILLIAM: Three times a week?

STEPHEN: Oh.

WILLIAM: Nobody likes the minimalists that much.

STEPHEN: No.

WILLIAM: Not even another minimalist.

STEPHEN: Mmn.
(*Pause*)
I've always liked the minimalists.

WILLIAM: Have you?

STEPHEN: Yes.

WILLIAM: I suppose they are rather funny.

STEPHEN: I think so, too.

(*Pause*)

WILLIAM: The rat.

STEPHEN: Yes.

WILLIAM: Whoever he is.

STEPHEN: Mmn.

WILLIAM: To try something like that.

STEPHEN: And succeed, yes.

(*Pause. William looks at him.*)

I mean, if he did.

WILLIAM: If he did?

STEPHEN: Succeed, I mean.

WILLIAM: Yes. He'd better be careful, whoever he is.

STEPHEN: Mmn.

WILLIAM: If he did, I mean.

STEPHEN: Yes.

(*Pause*)

The thing is, he could turn out to be quite a nice fellow.

WILLIAM: I wouldn't be surprised.

STEPHEN: Especially if Christine likes him.

WILLIAM: She probably likes him because she feels sorry for him.

STEPHEN: Do you think so?

WILLIAM: Yes.
(*Pause*)

STEPHEN: What if she loves him?

WILLIAM: Stephen.

STEPHEN: I'm sorry. I was just thinking ahead.

WILLIAM: Thinking ahead.

STEPHEN: Preparing you for the shock.

WILLIAM: The shock?

STEPHEN: The worst. Just in case, I mean.
(*Pause*)
I'm sorry.

WILLIAM: You're not acting very sympathetic.

STEPHEN: No, I'm not. I'm sorry.

WILLIAM: In fact, you seem faintly amused.

STEPHEN: I'm not. Really.

WILLIAM: No?

STEPHEN: Of course not.
(*Pause. Stephen laughs.*)
Sorry. I'm sorry.

WILLIAM: *I* know why you're having such a good time.

STEPHEN (*Worried*): You do?

WILLIAM: You already told me.

STEPHEN: I did?

WILLIAM: It's because you're in love.

STEPHEN: Oh.
(*Pause*)
Yes.

WILLIAM: Congratulations.

STEPHEN: Thank you.

WILLIAM: It's wonderful.

STEPHEN: Thanks.

WILLIAM: When can I meet her?

STEPHEN: Sooner than you think.

WILLIAM: That would be nice.

STEPHEN: Yes.

WILLIAM: She's not anything like Liz is she?

STEPHEN: Not really, no.

WILLIAM: That's good.

STEPHEN: Mmn.

WILLIAM: You needed a change.

STEPHEN: Yes.
(*Pause*)
She's more . . . she's more like Christine, actually.

WILLIAM: *Is* she?

STEPHEN: Yes.

WILLIAM: Well, *that* should be interesting.

STEPHEN: In what way?

WILLIAM: Well, in almost every way, I guess.
(*Pause*)
Where did you meet her?
(*Pause*)

STEPHEN: At the Museum of Modern Art.

WILLIAM: You're kidding.

STEPHEN: No.

WILLIAM: Really?

STEPHEN: Yes.

WILLIAM: At the minimalist exhibit?

STEPHEN: Mmn.

WILLIAM: My God.

STEPHEN: Incredible, isn't it?

WILLIAM: How do you like that.

STEPHEN: Yes.
(*Pause*)

WILLIAM: There aren't any problems, are there?

STEPHEN: Well, actually, there are a few, yes.

WILLIAM: Like what?

STEPHEN: Like, well . . .

WILLIAM: She's not engaged or anything, is she?

STEPHEN: No, of course not.

WILLIAM: That's good.
(*Pause*)

STEPHEN: Well, she is, in fact. Yes.

(*Pause*)

WILLIAM: Stephen.

STEPHEN: Yes.

WILLIAM: Not really.

STEPHEN: Mmn.

WILLIAM: My God.

STEPHEN: I'm afraid so.

WILLIAM: You *do* set yourself up for things.

STEPHEN: I guess.

WILLIAM: No wonder you've been having trouble seeing things from my point of view!

STEPHEN: What do you mean?

WILLIAM: Well, just look at the position you're in!

STEPHEN: Oh.

(*Pause*)

Yes.

WILLIAM: What are you going to do?

STEPHEN: I don't know. I feel terrible. The thing is, we've fallen hopelessly in love with each other. I've decided . . . to keep her for myself.

WILLIAM: Has she told her fiancé?

STEPHEN: Not yet. But he'll just have to be made to understand.

WILLIAM: You think so?

STEPHEN: We're talking about love, after all.

WILLIAM: We are?

STEPHEN: Well, aren't we?

WILLIAM: I suppose so. Yes.
(*Pause*)
She's not leading you on, is she?

STEPHEN: Leading me on?

WILLIAM: She's not doing it just to have a good time, is she?

STEPHEN: I don't think . . .

WILLIAM: A final fling before the big step . . .

STEPHEN: No.

WILLIAM: Because I know how involved you become, and I'd hate to see you get upset.

STEPHEN: Upset?

WILLIAM: Disappointed. If things didn't work out.
(*Pause*)
Be careful, Stephen.

STEPHEN: I will.

WILLIAM: I'd have it out with her fiancé.

STEPHEN: Mmn.

WILLIAM: I'd talk to her, too, if I were you.
(*Pause*)

STEPHEN: Yes.
(*Pause. Sophia Pickle re-enters.*)

SOPHIA: Here you go.

STEPHEN: Thank you.

SOPHIA (*To William*): Sure you don't want anything?

STEPHEN: We'll share this.

SOPHIA: How about dessert?

STEPHEN: How about a menu?

SOPHIA: Chocolate sundae, hold the cherry?

STEPHEN: Not today.
(*Pause*)

SOPHIA: You still looking, then?
(*Pause*)

STEPHEN: Yes.

(*Blackout*)

SCENE FOUR

(*At the Opera. Same box. Christine seated between Stephen and William, her hand in William's. Same Man and Woman in front.*)

CHRISTINE: What a mess this is.

STEPHEN: What?

CHRISTINE: This. It's a mess, isn't it?

STEPHEN: I don't think so.

CHRISTINE: You don't?

STEPHEN: Not at all. It's very exciting.

CHRISTINE: Well, Yes . . .

STEPHEN: And certainly tragic.

CHRISTINE: You think so?

STEPHEN: Especially for poor Violetta.

CHRISTINE: Oh. Yes.

(*Pause*)

I wasn't talking about the opera.

STEPHEN: You weren't?

CHRISTINE: No.

STEPHEN: Oh.

CHRISTINE: I was talking about *us*.

STEPHEN: What *about* us?

CHRISTINE: *You* know.

STEPHEN: Oh. Yes.

(*Beams*)

WILLIAM: What's the matter, aren't you two enjoying this?

STEPHEN: Yes!

WILLIAM: Oh.

CHRISTINE: No. Not especially. No. Not at all.

(*Woman, Man, Stephen, William, Christine exchange glances.*)

WILLIAM: Maybe you and I should change places.

STEPHEN: Why?

WILLIAM: You can see better from where I'm sitting.

STEPHEN: You can?

WILLIAM: Yes. Let's.

STEPHEN: It's—oh, I'm all right.

WILLIAM: Are you sure?

STEPHEN: *Yes.*

WILLIAM: All right.

STEPHEN: Thanks, anyway.

WILLIAM: Not at all.

STEPHEN (*To Christine*): When can I see you?

CHRISTINE: Tomorrow.

STEPHEN: All right. Have you got a piece of paper?

CHRISTINE: No.

STEPHEN: How about a pen?

(*Christine hands Stephen pen. He writes. Woman turns. Sees Stephen. Turns back.*)

WOMAN: Have you a piece of paper?

MAN: Sorry.

WOMAN: May I borrow a pen?

(*Aria ends. Applause*)

MAN: Brava! Bravissima! Brava!

WOMAN: Brava!

MAN: Such vibrato, such a range! She was even better tonight than a month ago. The best I've ever seen her!

WOMAN: Which one was she?

MAN: Ortenzia?

WOMAN: Yes.

MAN: The one who just walked off.

WOMAN: The one who coughed to death?

MAN: The one who coughed to death and just walked off.
(*Pause*)
She's coming back again.

WILLIAM: Bravo!

WOMAN: Excuse me, Monsieur?

STEPHEN: Yes?

WOMAN: I believe you dropped this.

STEPHEN: I did?

WOMAN: Yes.
(*She hands him note.*)

STEPHEN: Thank you.

(*To Christine*)

Excuse me, Mademoiselle . . .

CHRISTINE: Yes?

STEPHEN: I believe you dropped this.

CHRISTINE: I did?

STEPHEN: Yes.

(*He hands her* HIS *note.*)

CHRISTINE: Thank you.

(*William turns back. Pause*)

WILLIAM: Who just gave her that note?

STEPHEN (*indicates Man*): He did.

WILLIAM: So! It's him, is it?

STEPHEN: I suppose so. Yes.

WILLIAM (*To Man*): Excuse me, sir.

MAN: Yes.

WILLIAM: I believe you dropped this.

(*Hands him program*)

MAN: I did?

WILLIAM: Yes.

MAN: Thank you.

(William punches the bewildered Man. Woman screams. Stephen grabs Christine. They rush out.)

(Blackout)

SCENE FIVE

(*Hotel suite. Christine, reading.*)

CHRISTINE: "Lotte had slept little that night. Everything she had feared had happened, in a manner which she had neither anticipated nor imagined . . . Was it the passions of Werther's embraces that reverberated through her heart? How was she to face Albert? They had not talked freely for so long . . ."

(*Pause*)

WILLIAM (*Offstage*): Room Service! Ready?

CHRISTINE: Yes.

WILLIAM: Close your eyes.

CHRISTINE: Do I have to?

WILLIAM: Mmn-hmn.

(*William enters, slightly drunk. Hands Christine champagne.*)

CHRISTINE: William!

WILLIAM: Your favorite.

CHRISTINE: Yes.

WILLIAM: We shall drink and dine till we can drink and dine no more.

CHRISTINE: That'll be nice.

WILLIAM: Cheers!

CHRISTINE: Cheers!

WILLIAM: To us!

CHRISTINE: To us. Yes.

(*Pause*)

WILLIAM: I can no longer help myself. I am in love with you. Sun, moon and stars may continue on their course, but for me there is neither day nor night, and the entire universe around me has ceased to exist.

CHRISTINE: William, are you all right?

WILLIAM: Don't I seem all right?

CHRISTINE: You seem a little drunk.

WILLIAM: I am a little drunk. I had a couple down in the Oak Room while I was waiting for you.

CHRISTINE: A couple of what?

WILLIAM: A couple of scotches.

CHRISTINE: William, you don't even drink!

WILLIAM: That's what I told them downstairs, yes.

(*Pause. William laughs. Christine looks at William, laughs.*)

This is a wonderful suite. Do you like it?

CHRISTINE: I adore it.

WILLIAM: I'm so glad I suggested it. It's wonderful, isn't it?

CHRISTINE: Yes.

(*Pause*)

How did you know to pick *this* suite?

WILLIAM: I'd stayed in it once before.

CHRISTINE: You did?

WILLIAM: Many years ago. Besides, Stephen recommended it.

CHRISTINE: Stephen?

WILLIAM: Apparently he stayed here recently.

CHRISTINE: He did?

WILLIAM: With his new girlfriend.

CHRISTINE: Is that what he told you?

WILLIAM: When I asked him.

CHRISTINE: And he said that he liked it?

WILLIAM: Very much.

(*Pause*)

Have you met her?

CHRISTINE: Who?

WILLIAM: His new girlfriend?

CHRISTINE: Not yet.

WILLIAM: He's told me all about her.

CHRISTINE: Has he?

WILLIAM: Mmn. He's head over heels in love with her, I think.

CHRISTINE: Is he?

WILLIAM: I think he's going to ask her to marry him.

CHRISTINE: Do you really?

WILLIAM: I think so. Yes.
(*William laughs.*)
Oops.

CHRISTINE: What's the matter?

WILLIAM: I just spilled . . .

CHRISTINE: Is it all right?

WILLIAM: It's fine. It's only champagne. It's fine. It's fine.

(*Pause. William touches Christine.*)

Christine . . .

CHRISTINE: Mmn?

WILLIAM: Are you all right?

CHRISTINE: Of course.

WILLIAM: You seem troubled.

CHRISTINE: I'm not.

WILLIAM: Are you sure?

CHRISTINE: Yes.
(*Pause*)

WILLIAM: I told you I was sorry about last night.

CHRISTINE: Mmn.

WILLIAM: It was all a terrible mistake.

CHRISTINE: I know.

WILLIAM: I'm glad I didn't actually hurt the man.

CHRISTINE: I'm glad they released him from the hospital.

WILLIAM: He was in shock more than anything, I think.

CHRISTINE: That must have been it.
(*Pause*)

WILLIAM: Still, it was pretty funny.

CHRISTINE: Mmn.

WILLIAM: If you could have seen his face.

CHRISTINE: Oh, God!

WILLIAM: What a riot!

CHRISTINE: Yes.
(*They laugh*)

WILLIAM: I can't believe Stephen.

CHRISTINE: No.

WILLIAM: Telling me that was the man.

CHRISTINE: Mmn.

WILLIAM: He goes too far sometimes, you know that?

CHRISTINE: Yes.
(*Pause*)

WILLIAM: He's impossible when he's in love.

CHRISTINE: I know.

WILLIAM: He gets everything confused.

CHRISTINE: Mmn.

WILLIAM: The rest of the world stops, except for him and his perfect woman. He forgets other people have real feelings, too. Have you ever noticed that?

CHRISTINE: I have, yes.

(*Pause*)

WILLIAM: Are you still thinking about him?

CHRISTINE: Stephen?

WILLIAM: No. Him. The other one.

CHRISTINE: The other one?

WILLIAM: The one *you're* in love with.

(*Pause*)

CHRISTINE: Oh. Him. Yes.

(*Pause*)

WILLIAM: I won't ask who he is, Christine.

CHRISTINE: No. Don't.

WILLIAM: I'd just like to know where things stand between us. If that's not too much to ask.

(*Pause*)

CHRISTINE: I'm confused.

WILLIAM: Yes.

CHRISTINE: I'm just confused.

WILLIAM: Mmn.

CHRISTINE: Something like this has never happened to me before.

WILLIAM: I know.

CHRISTINE: But it just happened, William. Nobody planned it. It just happened.

WILLIAM (*Pause*): Is it very different when you're with him?

CHRISTINE: Very.

WILLIAM: Nicer?

CHRISTINE: Different.

WILLIAM: But if you had to choose . . .

CHRISTINE: William, I don't want to choose!

WILLIAM: You may not want to, but you're going to have to, Christine . . .

CHRISTINE: Yes, I know that William. Yes!
(*Pause. Christine spills champagne on William.*)

WILLIAM: Oops.

CHRISTINE: Oh God.

WILLIAM: You spilled.

CHRISTINE: I'm sorry.

WILLIAM: Maybe I better take them off.

CHRISTINE: Maybe you'd better.

WILLIAM: I'll take them off.
(*Pause*)
I'm sorry.

CHRISTINE: It was my fault.

WILLIAM: No, it wasn't. Now I've blown it.

CHRISTINE: No, you haven't.

WILLIAM: Yes, I have. Now I've lost you. I have lost you, haven't I?
(*Pause*)
Have I lost you?

CHRISTINE: Oh, William, of course not.

WILLIAM: I have.

CHRISTINE: You haven't.
(*Pause*)

WILLIAM: Is it because I'm boring?

CHRISTINE: You're not boring.

WILLIAM: I am. Let's face it.

CHRISTINE: William, if you're boring, then I'm boring.

WILLIAM: Sometimes you can be pretty boring. "Love Rites of the Yanomamo."

CHRISTINE: You love reading about the Yanomamo!

WILLIAM: Yes, well, so do you!

CHRISTINE: No, I don't. I find it boring.

WILLIAM: You see!

CHRISTINE: Only because it's my work!

WILLIAM: You love your work!

CHRISTINE: Well, yes. I do! I love my work.
(*William laughs. Christine laughs.*)

WILLIAM: Maybe you'd better lie down.

CHRISTINE: Maybe *you'd* better lie down.

WILLIAM: I think we should both lie down.

CHRISTINE: Why don't *you* just lie down?

WILLIAM: No, you should, too.

CHRISTINE: You think so?

WILLIAM: Yes.
(*Pause. They lie down.*)

CHRISTINE: I do like you.

WILLIAM: Do you?

CHRISTINE: Very much.

WILLIAM: Do you love me?

CHRISTINE: Yes.
(*Pause*)

WILLIAM: Will you marry me?

CHRISTINE: What?

WILLIAM: If I asked you?
(*Pause*)

CHRISTINE: Are you asking me?

WILLIAM: Yes.
(*Pause*)
Will you marry me?
(*Pause*)
Marry me, Christine.
(*Pause*)

CHRISTINE: This is all happening a little suddenly, isn't it?

WILLIAM: Is it?

CHRISTINE: I mean, we've waited so long for this, and now . . .

WILLIAM: It's happened. It's just happened.

CHRISTINE: Yes.
(*Pause*)

WILLIAM: When will you tell him?

CHRISTINE: I don't know. I can't.

WILLIAM: You can. The next time you see him. I'll come with you.

CHRISTINE: No, I don't want you to meet him.

WILLIAM: I don't want you to get hurt.

CHRISTINE: I won't.

WILLIAM: Are you sure?

CHRISTINE: Yes.

(*Pause*)

WILLIAM: I do love you. Very much.

CHRISTINE: I know that.

WILLIAM: And I'll be good for you. We'll be good for each other. I'll take care of you. Do you know that?

CHRISTINE: Yes.

(*Pause. William laughs.*)

What is it?

WILLIAM: I was just thinking. About the Yanomama.

CHRISTINE: The Yanomamo. Yes.

(*Blackout*)

SCENE SIX

(*At the Museum of Modern Art. Stephen and Christine looking at painting.*)

CHRISTINE: Where's the point?

STEPHEN: What's the point?

CHRISTINE: *Where's* the point.

STEPHEN: Right *there*. The two lines intersect at the circle. Otherwise, they never touch.

CHRISTINE: I don't think I understand it.

STEPHEN: There's not much to understand.

CHRISTINE: There isn't?

STEPHEN: No.

CHRISTINE: It doesn't excite me.

STEPHEN: It's not supposed to.

CHRISTINE: It's not?

STEPHEN: No. It's supposed to make you think.

CHRISTINE: If I wanted to think, I'd read a book.

STEPHEN: What's wrong with looking at a painting?

CHRISTINE: It makes me feel stupid.
(*Pause*)

STEPHEN: I think it's rather funny, actually.

CHRISTINE: Do you?

STEPHEN: Yes.
(*Pause*)

CHRISTINE: Let's go out to the sculpture garden.

STEPHEN: Do you want to?

CHRISTINE: Mmn.

STEPHEN: It's wet out there, isn't it?

CHRISTINE: It's letting up.

STEPHEN: All right.
(*They start out*)
Wait, Christine.
(*Christine stops. Stephen looks around. Then kisses her*)

CHRISTINE: Silly.

STEPHEN: I like to.

CHRISTINE: The guard is looking at us.

STEPHEN: He doesn't care.
(*They kiss.*)

CHRISTINE: Come on.
(*They exit.*)

(*Blackout*)

SCENE SEVEN

(*The sculpture garden.*)

CHRISTINE: It's nice out here, isn't it?

STEPHEN: Yes. I think it's starting to rain. Christine, do you remember the first day we talked?

CHRISTINE: We went to the Park afterward.

STEPHEN: The three of us.

CHRISTINE: Yes.

STEPHEN: And William and you went to the zoo.

CHRISTINE: And you wrote me a note in "The Sorrows of Young Werther."

STEPHEN: You'd left the book on the bench.

CHRISTINE: I did?

STEPHEN: Yes.

CHRISTINE: How did you know?

STEPHEN: I saw you.

CHRISTINE: You did?

STEPHEN: I was hiding in the bushes.

CHRISTINE: You were?

STEPHEN: Yes.

CHRISTINE: And what did I do?

STEPHEN: You came back and read it.

CHRISTINE: And then?

STEPHEN: You left.

CHRISTINE: And what did you do?

STEPHEN: I followed you. And later that afternoon, we kissed. For the very first time.

CHRISTINE: I remember that. Yes.

(*Pause*)

STEPHEN: It seems like such a long time ago.

CHRISTINE: A month?

STEPHEN: Two.

CHRISTINE: *Two* months?

STEPHEN: To the day, in fact.

CHRISTINE: It seems shorter.

STEPHEN: It's been a long time.

CHRISTINE: Like it was such a short time ago.
(*Pause*)

STEPHEN: I brought you something.

CHRISTINE: You did?

STEPHEN: Close your eyes.

CHRISTINE: Do I have to?

STEPHEN: Mmn-hmn.
(*She does. He places an orange in her hand.*)

CHRISTINE: Stephen.

STEPHEN: Yes.

CHRISTINE: Thank you.
(*They embrace. Pause*)
Oh, God.

STEPHEN: What's the matter?

CHRISTINE: Oh, it's nothing. No.
(*Pause*)

STEPHEN: I'm sorry about the other night.

CHRISTINE: It's all right.

STEPHEN: There was nothing else I could do.

CHRISTINE: Of course. I know.

(*Pause*)

STEPHEN: William certainly seemed very upset about the whole thing, didn't he.

CHRISTINE: He did. Yes.

STEPHEN: Well, now he knows.

CHRISTINE: Mmn.

STEPHEN: But he doesn't know *who* . . .

CHRISTINE: No.

(*Pause*)

STEPHEN: Christine, I've been thinking . . .

CHRISTINE: So have I, Stephen.

STEPHEN: We must tell William everything. We must declare our love for each other openly.

CHRISTINE: We can't, Stephen.

STEPHEN: We can't?

CHRISTINE: No.

STEPHEN: Why not?

CHRISTINE: It won't work.

STEPHEN: You think he'll get angry?

CHRISTINE: It's not that.

STEPHEN: You think he won't understand?

CHRISTINE: I'm not talking about him.

STEPHEN: You're not?

CHRISTINE: I'm talking about us.

STEPHEN: Oh.

CHRISTINE: Yes.
(*Pause*)

STEPHEN: The three of us?

CHRISTINE: The two of us.

STEPHEN: You and me?

CHRISTINE: Yes.

STEPHEN: Oh.
(*Pause*)

CHRISTINE: Stephen.

STEPHEN: I don't understand.

CHRISTINE: I know.

STEPHEN: Why can't we . . .

CHRISTINE: It won't work.

STEPHEN: Why not?

CHRISTINE: Because.

STEPHEN: Oh, God.

CHRISTINE: I think we should go back in.

STEPHEN: Christine . . .

CHRISTINE: It's beginning to rain.

STEPHEN: You're not angry with me, are you?

CHRISTINE: Of course not.

STEPHEN: You are.

CHRISTINE: I'm not.

STEPHEN: Are you sure?

CHRISTINE: Yes.

STEPHEN: Then what are we going to do?

CHRISTINE: About what?

STEPHEN: About us.

CHRISTINE: I don't know.

STEPHEN: For how long do you think . . .

CHRISTINE: Stephen, I'm engaged!

STEPHEN: But I love you!

CHRISTINE: I know.

STEPHEN: Maybe we could run away together.

CHRISTINE: What?

STEPHEN: You and I.

CHRISTINE: But I love William!

STEPHEN: But you love me, too!

CHRISTINE: I do! Yes!

STEPHEN: Well . . .

CHRISTINE: Oh, my God, I don't know . . . Oh, Stephen, we should never have gotten involved with each other!

STEPHEN: Don't say that!

CHRISTINE: It's true!

STEPHEN: Why did we?

CHRISTINE: I don't know!

STEPHEN: We did it because we love each other!

CHRISTINE: Yes.

STEPHEN: Because you find me attractive and diffident and fun to be with . . .

CHRISTINE: Yes . . .

STEPHEN: You weren't making all that up, were you, Christine?

CHRISTINE: No!

STEPHEN: Then marry me.

CHRISTINE: What?

STEPHEN: Marry *me*.

CHRISTINE: Stephen.

STEPHEN: Come away with me.
(*Pause*)

CHRISTINE: I can't, Stephen.

STEPHEN: Please.
(*Pause*)

CHRISTINE: Oh, Stephen, I'm sorry. I'm so sorry. I can't . . . Stephen . . . No.
(*Pause*)

William has asked me to marry him. Last night. We're going to go away together.
(*Pause*)

STEPHEN: Oh, my God. Oh, my God. Oh, my God. Oh.

(*Pause*)

So he's going to do it.

CHRISTINE: Yes.

STEPHEN: So he's finally going to do it.

CHRISTINE: Mmn.

STEPHEN: And you're going to do it with him.

CHRISTINE: I suppose so.

STEPHEN: And all of this has been brought about by me.

CHRISTINE: We do love each other, Stephen.

STEPHEN: Yes, of course. I know.

(*Pause*)

It's what you've wanted all along, isn't it?

CHRISTINE: What?

STEPHEN: To marry William. I never did stand a chance, did I?

CHRISTINE: Stephen, what are you saying?

STEPHEN: William's been the one you've loved, and William's been the one you've wanted.

CHRISTINE: It hasn't been that simple, Stephen!

STEPHEN: Hasn't it?

CHRISTINE: No!

(*Pause*)

STEPHEN: William was right, you know.

CHRISTINE: About what?

STEPHEN: He said something like this might happen.

CHRISTINE: He did?

STEPHEN: He said whoever it was might be leading me on.

CHRISTINE: I didn't do that, Stephen.

STEPHEN: Didn't you?

CHRISTINE: We knew what we were getting ourselves into.

STEPHEN: But I was willing to take this all the way.

CHRISTINE: Yes, well, I was, too.

STEPHEN: Then why are you leaving me, Christine?

CHRISTINE: Because I want William.

STEPHEN: I thought you wanted me!

CHRISTINE: I thought I did, too! Oh, Stephen, I love you both! But I can't have you both! And William and I are right for each other.

STEPHEN: And we're not?

CHRISTINE: Of course we are! But not *as* right!

STEPHEN: We're talking about love, Christine, not an editorial decision!

CHRISTINE: Stephen, please don't take this personally!

STEPHEN: Who else is it happening to?

CHRISTINE: I'm not what you've been looking for, Stephen.

STEPHEN: Christine, you are my perfect woman!

CHRISTINE: I wouldn't always be what you'd want me to!
(*Pause*)

STEPHEN: *ARRRRGHHHH!*
(*Pause*)

CHRISTINE: I wish there was something I could tell you.

STEPHEN: Like what?

CHRISTINE: Like that I love you and I wish things could be different.

STEPHEN: You could tell me that.

CHRISTINE: Would it help?

STEPHEN: It might.

CHRISTINE: I love you and I wish things could be different.

STEPHEN: It didn't help.

CHRISTINE: I'm sorry.

(*Pause*)

I wish things *could* be different, Stephen. Maybe they will for you next time.

STEPHEN: I was hoping that *this* might have been different, Christine.

CHRISTINE: Yes. I know.

(*Pause*)

STEPHEN: Is it over then?

CHRISTINE: I'm afraid so.

STEPHEN: Then there's no hope of . . .

CHRISTINE: No.

STEPHEN: Then you'd better go.

(*Pause*)

CHRISTINE: Are you sure you're all right?

STEPHEN: I don't know.

CHRISTINE: Stephen.

STEPHEN: I feel a little funny.

CHRISTINE: A little funny?

STEPHEN: A little lost. As if something terrible were about to happen.

CHRISTINE: Something terrible?

STEPHEN: Something awkward.

CHRISTINE: Like what?

STEPHEN: I don't know.

CHRISTINE: Stephen . . .

STEPHEN: It is really over?

CHRISTINE: Yes.

STEPHEN: And there's no hope of . . .

CHRISTINE: No.

STEPHEN: Then you'd better go.

CHRISTINE: Are you sure . . .

STEPHEN: Christine, please! *Go!*

(*Christine starts out. Then she turns back. Goes to him. Embraces him. They kiss. William enters. Goes to Stephen. Turns him round. Socks him in nose. Stephen falls.*)

CHRISTINE: William.

WILLIAM: Christ!

CHRISTINE: Yes.

WILLIAM: Stephen!

CHRISTINE: Yes.

WILLIAM: Oh, my God!

CHRISTINE: Yes.
(*Pause*)

WILLIAM: Oh.
(*Pause*)

                    (*Blackout*)

SCENE EIGHT

(*The taxi. Stephen and William in the back seat. Ginny Tremaine behind the wheel. Stephen has patch on his nose.*)

WILLIAM: You'll have to forget about her, Stephen.

STEPHEN: How can I?

WILLIAM: You must.

STEPHEN: But I've fallen in love with her!

WILLIAM: I know.

STEPHEN: I love her more than I've ever loved anybody!

WILLIAM: Stephen.

STEPHEN: I'm sorry, William. I do.

WILLIAM: Love for Christine may mean many things. But it's not the same as marriage.

STEPHEN: Christine doesn't need to be married.

WILLIAM: She does.

STEPHEN: Well then *I'll* marry her!

WILLIAM: We need each other, Stephen.

STEPHEN: Yes.

WILLIAM: We need each other very much.

STEPHEN: I know.
(*Pause*)

WILLIAM: The nose still hurt?

STEPHEN: The throbbing's stopped.

WILLIAM: The pain still there?

STEPHEN: It's tender.

WILLIAM: It'll take a while.

STEPHEN: Yes.
(*Pause*)

WILLIAM: Are you all right?
(*Stephen shrugs.*)
What are you going to . . .

STEPHEN: I don't know.

WILLIAM: We wouldn't want you to . . .

STEPHEN: I wouldn't want to, no.

WILLIAM: Maybe you could . . .

STEPHEN: I wouldn't like that, either.

WILLIAM: Well then how about . . .

STEPHEN: No.
(*Pause*)

WILLIAM: Are you sure you're all right?
(*Stephen shrugs.*)
Stephen, you wouldn't try anything foolish . . .

STEPHEN: I might! I might! I don't know!
(*Pause*)

GINNY: This okay?

STEPHEN: Fine. Thank you.

WILLIAM: Would you like to spend the night with us?

STEPHEN: No.

WILLIAM: Should I tell Christine . . .

STEPHEN: I'm all right.

WILLIAM: I'm sure she feels bad.

STEPHEN: Yes.

WILLIAM: I'll call you.

STEPHEN: See you.

WILLIAM: Are you sure . . .

STEPHEN: I'm all right, William! Let me go!
(*He gets out.*)

GINNY: (*Hands him copy of* The Sorrows of Young Werther):
By the way, you left this. The last time.

STEPHEN: I did?

GINNY: Thanks.

STEPHEN: Sure.

GINNY: It's wonderful, isn't it.

STEPHEN: No!
(*Stephen exits.*)

GINNY: Will he be all right?

WILLIAM: I hope so.

GINNY: New girlfriend, huh?

WILLIAM: Old one, I'm afraid.

GINNY: The new ones become old ones.

WILLIAM: Yes.

GINNY: "Così fan tutte."

WILLIAM: Pardon?

GINNY: So do they all.
(*Pause*)
Where to?

WILLIAM: Three blocks west.

GINNY: Tell me when.
(*She starts up.*)

(*Blackout*)

SCENE NINE

(*Stephen at his desk writing letter.*)

STEPHEN: Dear Christine: Is it ourselves or our circumstances that conspire against us? Somehow I wish I knew . . . For a while I dreamed that love might continue between us. But now that dream will die from the same impossibility that marked the love of Werther for Lotte in *The Sorrows of You-Know-Who* . . .

(*Tears paper. Crumples it. Tosses it away. Starts again*)

My dear Christine: By the time you read this, peace shall have come to the unfortunate friend whose last deed was addressed to the woman he loved but could not keep. Having suffered enough in this life, I pray for the time when we shall be locked in an infinite, eternal embrace in the next . . .

(*Tears paper. Crumples it. Starts again*)

My dearest, darling Christine . . .

(*Tears paper*)

Christine: There is no hope. See pages 220–221, especially the last three lines. Love, Stephen . . .

(*Folds letter. Places it in envelope. Considers for a moment. Opens desk drawer. Takes out gun seen in first two scenes. Con-*

siders. Aims it at his temple. Considers. Puts it to his mouth. Considers. Opens copy of The Sorrows of Young Werther. *Reads.*)

". . . He had shot himself through the head above the right eye, and his brain was laid bare. He had then slid down and rolled around the chair in convulsions. He had drunk only one glass of red wine . . ."

(*He goes to cabinet. Pours himself glass of wine. Drinks. Goes back to desk. Cocks trigger. Holds gun to head. Pause. Doorbell rings.*)

Christ!

(*Furious knocking. Stephen goes to door.*)

Go away!

CHRISTINE (*Off*): I won't!

STEPHEN: I'm not going to open up!

CHRISTINE: I'll call the police if you don't!

STEPHEN: Christine!

CHRISTINE: Stephen!

STEPHEN: No!

CHRISTINE: *Yes!*

STEPHEN: Oh . . .

(*Stephen sighs. Puts gun back in drawer. Goes to door. Admits Christine. Pause*)

CHRISTINE: I came to tell you I'm sorry.

STEPHEN: Mmn.

CHRISTINE: I am.

STEPHEN: Yes.

CHRISTINE: I tried calling you all morning.

STEPHEN: I know.

CHRISTINE: I came knocking on your door.

STEPHEN: I thought it was you.

CHRISTINE: I didn't sleep a wink all night.

STEPHEN: Neither did I.

CHRISTINE: I was worried sick about you.
(*Pause*)
Oh, Stephen.

STEPHEN: Yes.

CHRISTINE: I think it will just take a little time.

STEPHEN: I don't care anymore.

CHRISTINE: Don't say that, Stephen!

STEPHEN: I don't!

CHRISTINE: You do!

STEPHEN: Go away, Christine! I don't want to see you again!

CHRISTINE: Stephen, please!

STEPHEN: Say what you have to say and go!

CHRISTINE: I just told you. I'm sorry!

STEPHEN: Fine, thank you!
(*Pause*)

CHRISTINE: Why are you being like this?

STEPHEN: Like what?

CHRISTINE: Like the way you're being.

STEPHEN: I'm sure I don't know.

CHRISTINE: Are you all right?

STEPHEN: I'm fine, yes.
(*Pause*)

CHRISTINE: Stop sulking.

STEPHEN: I'm not sulking.

CHRISTINE: You are.

STEPHEN: I'm not.

CHRISTINE: Well, don't.

STEPHEN: I won't.

CHRISTINE: Stop it!

STEPHEN: No!

(*Pause*)

CHRISTINE: What's this?

STEPHEN: Don't touch it.

CHRISTINE: What is it?

STEPHEN: A letter.

CHRISTINE: Can I read it?

STEPHEN: Of course not.

CHRISTINE: But it's addressed to me.

STEPHEN: It isn't.

CHRISTINE: It says, "Dear Christine . . ."

STEPHEN: It's another Christine.

CHRISTINE: There's another Christine?

STEPHEN: There was, once.

CHRISTINE: Stephen, stop this!

STEPHEN: No!

CHRISTINE: You're being childish!

STEPHEN: And what are you being?

CHRISTINE: I'm trying to apologize to you.

STEPHEN: You already did. Now go!

CHRISTINE: Not until you tell me what's the matter with you!

STEPHEN: What's the matter with me?! What do you think?

CHRISTINE: I think you're enjoying acting hurt.

STEPHEN: I may be acting hurt, but I'm not enjoying it.

CHRISTINE: You're not?

STEPHEN: No!

CHRISTINE: Then why did you write me this letter?

STEPHEN: So you'd find it and read it.

CHRISTINE: Well, I found it . . .

STEPHEN: You can't read it . . .

CHRISTINE: Why not?

STEPHEN: It's too early yet.

CHRISTINE: Too early for what?

STEPHEN: Too early for this!
(*Produces gun*)

CHRISTINE: Oh, my God!

STEPHEN: Yes!

CHRISTINE: Oh!

(*Pause*)

Stephen . . .

STEPHEN: Yes . . .

CHRISTINE: My God.

STEPHEN: Go away, Christine.

CHRISTINE: Stephen . . .

STEPHEN: Go away . . .

CHRISTINE: No!

STEPHEN: You think I'm not serious about this?

CHRISTINE: I think you're very serious about this!

STEPHEN: Well then . . .

CHRISTINE: But there's no need to be *ridiculous* about it . . .

STEPHEN: *I'm not being ridiculous!*

CHRISTINE: Then don't shoot!

STEPHEN: I will!

CHRISTINE: Don't!

STEPHEN: Close your eyes!

CHRISTINE: Stephen!

STEPHEN: Christine!

CHRISTINE: No!

(*Click. Stephen fires the gun. It doesn't go off. Pause. Christine turns and looks at him. Stephen points the gun half into the air, and fires. BLAM! The gun goes off. Stephen spins and throws the gun onto his desk. He stands shaking as Christine rushes to him.*)

Stephen! Are you all right?

STEPHEN: Yes.

CHRISTINE: Are you sure?

STEPHEN: Yes.

CHRISTINE: Oh, my God.

STEPHEN: Yes.

CHRISTINE: Oh.

(*Pause. Stephen sits. Christine embraces him. Kisses him. He sits shaking. He sighs.*)

STEPHEN: Why do these things happen to me, Christine?

CHRISTINE: I don't know.

(*Pause. Christine laughs. Stephen looks at her, laughs.*)

STEPHEN: This whole thing has been a bit of a disaster, hasn't it?

CHRISTINE: A bit, yes.

STEPHEN: I'm afraid so. I think I hit the ficus.

(*Pause*)

Oh well, then. Oh, well.

(*Pause*)

CHRISTINE: What are you going to do?

STEPHEN: I don't know. I suppose I might move to the country for a while.

CHRISTINE: That would be nice.

STEPHEN: Or turn celibate. Maybe homosexual. Something that might, you know, make a slight difference.

CHRISTINE: I don't think you could do that, Stephen.

STEPHEN: You don't?

CHRISTINE: Not really.

STEPHEN: No. Neither do I. No.

(*Pause*)

CHRISTINE: Are you sure you're all right?

STEPHEN: No. But I will be.

CHRISTINE: Soon?

STEPHEN: I hope.

(*Pause*)

My love.

(*They kiss.*)

STEPHEN: So. You're leaving.

CHRISTINE: Yes.

STEPHEN: To where?

CHRISTINE: Someplace. I don't know.

STEPHEN: Have a nice wedding.

CHRISTINE: I will.

STEPHEN: I hope you'll be happy, Christine.

CHRISTINE: Yes, well. I hope so, too.
(*Pause*)
William feels bad.

STEPHEN: I'll call him.

CHRISTINE: Please call him.

STEPHEN: I'll tell him I'm all right.

CHRISTINE: Please. Do.
(*Pause*)
By the way. I finished it.

STEPHEN: Keep it.

CHRISTINE: Could I?

STEPHEN: Of course.

CHRISTINE: Thank you. I'd better go.

STEPHEN: Mmn.

(*Pause*)

CHRISTINE: Good-bye.

STEPHEN: Good-bye . . . my love.

(*She exits. Stephen watches her. Pause. He stands, signs. Considers. Goes and picks up new book. Opens it. Reads.*)

". . . She sat in the middle of the bench, quite alone. At least, dazzled by the light from her eyes, he perceived no one else. She raised her head as he passed, and involuntarily, he bowed; when he had gone a little farther, he stopped and looked back. She was like a vision . . ."

(*Pause. He stands. Goes to his desk. Finds note. Reads.*)

"Sorry I missed you the last time. My husband works at the Plaza. I'll see you Tuesday at the Pierre. Your friend at the opera, Emma Plante. (Mrs.)" Emma Plante . . . Mrs. X . . .

(*He goes to the phone and dials, deliberately, slowly.*)

Hello . . . Is this the Pierre? Yes, good afternoon. I'd like to make a reservation for two in the Yellowbird Room for this evening. Yes . . . The name? Hurt. Stephen Hurt. Hurt as in . . .

(*Pause*)

Yes, I'm afraid so. Well, thank you. See you then. Thank you.

(*He puts down receiver slowly. Stands staring straight ahead. Pause*)

(*Blackout*)

SCENE TEN

(*City street. Howard Fishbein [Bum] hailing a taxi. Well dressed. Clean looking. Carrying Stephen's umbrella. Rain.*)

BUM: Taxi! Hey, taxi! I'm going to be late! *Taxi!* Hey, *taxi!*

(*Car horn. Splash. He jumps back.*)

Jesus *Christ!*

(*Car horn. Bum shouts front.*)

Same to you!

(*Stephen enters.*)

STEPHEN: Want to share a cab?

BUM: Well, yes, if we can get one . . . Stephen! Stephen Hurt!

STEPHEN: Howard?

BUM: Yes!

STEPHEN: How are you?

BUM: Fine. You?

STEPHEN: Fine. Fine.

BUM: That's good.

STEPHEN: You're looking very well.

BUM: Thanks. So are you.

STEPHEN: Have you been working?

BUM: I sold my stories!

STEPHEN: You did?

BUM: Yes.

STEPHEN: Congratulations.

BUM: Thank you.

STEPHEN: That's wonderful.

BUM: Thanks.

STEPHEN: So you're writing?

BUM: I'm at work on a novel.

STEPHEN: That's wonderful, too.

(*Pause*)

BUM: Say, isn't this the book you suggested I read?

STEPHEN: Oh, yes.

BUM: It's wonderful, isn't it?

STEPHEN: Mmn.

BUM: Are you still reading it?

STEPHEN: No, this is Balzac. "Lost Illusions."

BUM: I'll have to read that, too.

STEPHEN: It's about this young man who falls madly in love with an older married woman.

BUM: Sounds wonderful.

STEPHEN: It is.

BUM: What happens?

STEPHEN: I don't know. I haven't gotten to the end yet.

BUM: *Taxi!* Hey, *taxi!*
(*Car horn*)
I can't be late. I'm meeting my wife for dinner.

STEPHEN: Marissa Himmelstein?

BUM: Yes. We're seeing each other again.

STEPHEN: That's wonderful.

BUM: It *is*, I guess. I wish I knew.

BOTH: TAXI!

(*Pause*)

STEPHEN: Oh, I nearly forgot. I've got something of yours back at the apartment.

BUM: Keep it, Stephen. I won't be needing it anymore.

STEPHEN: Neither will I.

BUM: Taxi!

STEPHEN: Let's go!

(*Squeal of brakes*)

BUM: Yes! Let's!

STEPHEN: After you . . .

(*Bum exits. Stephen waits just a moment. Tucks his book under his arm. Turns up his collar. Shoves his hands in his pockets, and saunters off to greet the new day.*)

(*Curtain*)

N.Y.C.—Hanover, N.H.—Gloucester,
Mass.—Baltimore, Md.—Stonington,
Ct.—Waterford, Ct.

1978–1980